PICTURE-PERFECT
escapes

Santa Barbara,
Ojai, Channel Islands &
the Santa Ynez Valley

HIDDEN

PICTURE-PERFECT
escapes

Santa Barbara,
Ojai, Channel Islands &
the Santa Ynez Valley

written and photographed by
Ellen Clark

Ulysses Press

Published by: Ulysses Press
P.O. Box 3440
Berkeley, CA 94703
www.ulyssespress.com

ISBN 1-56975-406-3
ISSN 1548-386X

Printed in Canada by Transcontinental Printing

10 9 8 7 6 5 4 3 2 1

Contributing writer: Keith Riegert
Design: Sarah Levin, Leslie Henriques
Editorial and production: Claire Chun, Lily Chou, Lee Micheaux, Steven Schwartz, Lynette Ubois
Maps: Pease Press
Index: Sayre Van Young

Photographs on pages 175 and 177 courtesy of Bacara Resort & Spa

Distributed in the United States by Publishers Group West and in Canada by Raincoast Books

Ulysses Press 🐢 is a federally registered trademark of BookPack, Inc.

WRITE TO US

If in your travels you discover a spot that captures the spirit of California's Central Coast, or if you live in the region and have a favorite place to share, or if you just feel like expressing your views, write to us and we'll pass your note along to the author.

We can't guarantee that the author will add your personal find to the next edition, but if the writer does use the suggestion, we'll acknowledge you in the credits and send you a free copy of the new edition.

ULYSSES PRESS
P.O. Box 3440
Berkeley, CA 94703
E-mail: readermail@ulyssespress.com

TABLE OF CONTENTS

1.

Santa Barbara
and Beyond

Twenty-five million years ago the North American and Pacific plates, sliding across the Earth's crust, slammed into one another off the central coast of California. The ensuing quakes thrust the sea floor above the ocean's grasp and created a new shelf of land, a new corner to an infant North America. The Spanish explorer Sebastian Vizcaino dropped anchor off this same curving, jagged coastline on Saint Barbara's Day, December 4, 1602. Though this did not mark the area's discovery, an honor grabbed by Juan Rodriguez Cabrillo in 1542, Vizcaino left his mark by naming the dusty, shrub-covered plain between the Pacific and the mountains after the patron saint of sailors, Santa Barbara.

Following these early visits Santa Barbara remained untouched for nearly a century. With the increase of trade throughout the Spanish Empire, the benefits of this coastal niche were finally recognized in 1782 with the establishment of Spain's final California Presidio. By 1793 a massive adobe fort enclosed an entire city block behind its walls, solidifying Spain's foothold on California's central coast.

When those first Spanish settlers arrived in Santa Barbara the land was already inhabited. The native Chumash Indians, who had settled the area nearly 6000 years before Cabrillo, had established a society intricately balanced with the sparse natural surroundings. About 20,000 to 30,000 Chumash were living in communities scattered across the Santa Barbara area, clustered around sources of fresh water. They had developed innovative ways of coping with survival in the harsh, coastal environment—living on a diet consisting of collected foodstuff such as acorns and herbs, grassland animals like squirrels, and most importantly, fish and shellfish harvested from the sea. Accomplished seafarers, the Chumash successfully navigated the Pacific from

Santa Barbara and Beyond

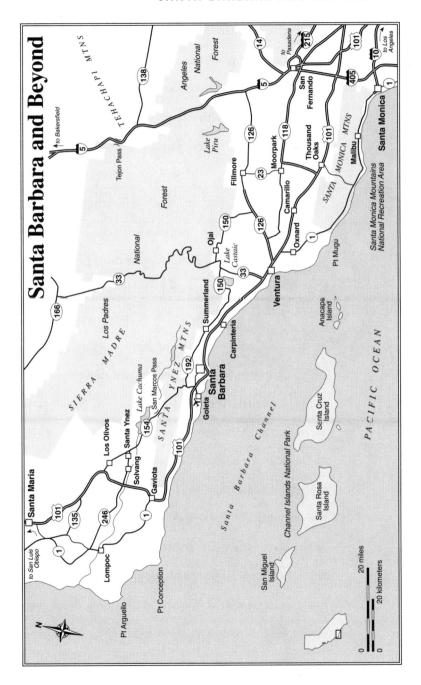

the Santa Barbara shore to the nearby Channel Islands in large planked canoes, carefully sealed with tar from the coast's natural petrol reserves.

With the arrival of Spanish soldiers and missionaries this peaceful lifestyle was shattered. Within a few years the Chumash population had been decimated and their unique culture had fallen to a new form of rule—Christianity.

En memoria de Dominga Muñoz

On Saint Barbara's day, December 4, 1786, a wooden cross was planted on the foundation of Santa Barbara's future Mission. Padre Fermin Lasuen held a dedication mass at the mission site. Although two destructive earthquakes contributed to the mission's 34-year building period, the Spanish Catholics were able to maintain control over the surrounding ranch lands and Chumash communities and by actively converting the Indians and forcing them into servitude the padres ran a self-sufficient operation until Spain lost control of Alta California during the Mexican Revolution of 1822.

As the 19th century ebbed, Santa Barbara began to show signs of radical transformation. The Mexican-American war, which ended in 1847, left all of Southern California under the rule of the United States and, following California's induction as a state in 1850, the dusty expanses of Spanish and Mexican *ranchos* gave way to Yankees moving west. In the late 1850s, as the San Francisco Gold Rush ushered a tidal wave of westward migration, Santa Barbara began to see a new kind of settler—the wealthy.

With the completion of the Los Angeles–Santa
Barbara railway line in 1887, this coastal retreat was
finally connected to Southern California. Fourteen
years later the city would link up with San Francisco and the rest of Northern California, and despite Santa Barbara's minor role in California's trade
industry, the rail connection ushered in a new era
for the town as a world-class travel destination.

With its delightful climate, this picture perfect get-away boasted some of North America's finest resorts and shopping opportunities; a description that has not changed in over a century.

As California grew in the early 1900s Santa Barbara saw its Mediterranean charm overlaid with the banal architecture of "modern" America. In frustration Santa Barbara's city planners pondered the city's architectural woes for a decade until the plates that had created the coastal shelf produced a shaky resolution. On June 19th, 1925, a massive earthquake destroyed the city's tacky downtown. Turning tragedy into triumph the citizens snatched the opportunity to transform the rubble of downtown into a Spanish-style metropolis linking its modern status as a beach mecca with its *ranchos* past. Replacing timber and concrete with adobe and red tile Santa Barbara emerged with the unique flavor of a city built to worship the sea and sun in exquisite style. Although the city has since teetered on the edge of a slide into the mundane suburban style of Southern California, it has not yet lost its charm. Tucked between the jagged peaks of the Coast Range and the deep waters of the Pacific, the town's Mediterranean flair is perfectly placed in this corner of California.

Today the sleepy yet upscale atmosphere of Santa Barbara has spread to its coastal and inland neighbors. Three main arteries, The Old Coast Route 1 and Routes 101 and 154, link Santa Barbara to surrounding towns. Traveling south along the shore, today's visitor sees rolling hills and steep bluffs that creep toward the waterfront, leaving just enough space for small beach towns like Carpinteria and Summerland and the quiet enclaves of Montecito and Ojai. East of Santa Barbara, amid chaparral-covered mountains, a booming wine industry

Fly Away Home

The California shore is one of the richest bird habitats anywhere in North America. Santa Barbara is strategically located on the Pacific flyway, that great migratory route spanning the western United States, and hundreds of species either migrate or live along the coastline here. Coastal bird species fall into three general categories—near-shore birds, like loons, grebes, cormorants, and scoters, that inhabit the shallow waters of bays and beaches; offshore birds, such as shearwaters, that feed several miles off the coast; and pelagic or open-ocean species, like albatross and Arctic terns, that fly miles from land and live for up to 20 or 30 years. Prime birding spots in the area include the Channel Islands, Goleta Beach County Park, and Andree Clark Bird Refuge.

has striped the Santa Ynez Valley with Tuscan vineyards and sunbaked wineries. To the north, the sleepy towns of Goleta, Solvang, and Lompoc still maintain something of their ranching and cowboy past.

Looking out over the city from Santa Barbara's foothills a patchwork of lanky palms and red roofs unfolds toward cobalt Pacific waters. From these vistas it's hard to grasp that this is a land scarred by conflict both on the surface and deep below. The region's history has been written by a collision of diverse cultures and tireless tectonic plates that still transform California's landscape. The centuries of struggle, destruction, and rebirth have delivered a

coastal stretch unlike any other in California. Today, while other areas succumb to high-rise expansion and endless urban sprawl, the towns and cities that comprise Santa Barbara's central coast strive to maintain the traditions of a rapidly fading past, a rich heritage that creates the foundation for a region rightly declared "picture perfect."

PACKING AND PREPARATION

Though weather in Santa Barbara is quite temperate—with winter temperatures ranging between an average high of 64 degrees (Fahrenheit) and a low of 45 degrees;

summer temperatures span a low of 60 and a high of 77—the sudden shifts in climate from midday to evening can feel extreme. Even a walk from the center of downtown to the beach can be a ten degree change. To cope with this uncertainty, especially during late spring and early summer when fog can be thick and damp, it's vital to dress in layers. Wear shorts in the summer but don't forget a long sleeve shirt; and as for winter, it may be Southern California, but don't let that fool you, the cold Pacific tends to spill cool air onto the coast.

Weather inland is quite a bit different. Without the ocean to keep temperatures mild the valleys boil over in the summer, often surpassing 100 degrees in the afternoon, and cooling to the mid 40s at night accompanied by heavy valley fog. So if you are planning to leave the coast pack for polarizing climates.

Rain is not a word easily found in Santa Barbara's vocabulary. Only 18 inches of rain fall on average in Santa Barbara, primarily concentrated between December and March, leaving most of the year dry and sunny. This dry almost desert climate poses one major concern to California—brush fires. During the fire season in the late summer and early autumn, before the first rains arrive, it's important to be vigilant when touring the backcountry and hiking through dried brush and grasslands. Fires occur often around this area and can move very quickly. In addition, keep in mind that Santa Barbara was created by violent earthquakes (with a major fault just north of Santa Barbara) and although most Californians seem jaded to these most common natural disasters, it's important to know the ins and outs of personal safety procedures—check evacuation routes and pack a flashlight and extra water.

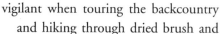

LODGING

Santa Barbara and her neighbors have no shortage of hotels, motels, and cozy inns. The neon signs of motels spread along the outskirts of Santa Barbara, upper State Street, and Goleta, and here is your best bet to economize (though in summer it might not appear that way), as long as you are willing to give up location and luxury. The waterfront, stretching from Montecito to the Mesa, boasts some of Santa Barbara's finest hotels with amenities inside, stellar views outside, and proximity to the city's major attractions. But don't look to the larger hotels for intimacy. In our opinion, the best of both worlds is met with the historic inns. With few rooms, inns and bed and breakfasts are able to sneak into residential areas, like Garden Street in Santa Barbara, and offer the traveler a unique view of city life. Many of these B&Bs provide home-cooked meals and afternoon snacks providing a perfect setting to meet other wanderers while making you feel a bit more comfortable away from home.

Deciding on a place to stay should be a compromise between taste and your pocketbook. To help you choose, we have described accommodations not only by area but price as well (prices are listed as double occupancy during the high season; note that rates tend to drop during the off season). *Budget* hotels are generally less than $60 per night for two people; the rooms are clean and comfortable, but not luxurious. *Moderate*-priced hotels run $60 to $120, and provide larger rooms, plusher furni-

Pockets of Life

Tidepools, exposed to view at low tide, are microcosms of the world. Delicately poised between land and sea, these rocky pockets are a frontier dividing two wildly varied environments. Life flourishes here, but living is not easy. Denizens of tidepools are exposed to air twice a day during low tide. They must adapt to dehydration, the heat of the sun, and the effects of the atmosphere. Rain brings fresh water to a saline environment, disturbing the precious equilibrium. Waves, particularly during severe storms, wreak havoc with reefs. Exceptionally high or low tides upset the rhythm of air and water exposure. This balance between time in the air and water differentiates tidal life forms. Tidepools, or intertidal areas, are divided into four zones, which parallel the beach and vary in their distance from shore. The splash zone, dampened by mist and occasional large waves, rests far up along the beach and is inhabited by green algae and small snails. Below it lies the upper intertidal zone, an area covered only during high tide. Here barnacles, chitons, and limpets cling to rocks, closing tight during low tide to preserve moisture. Covered by water twice a day, the middle intertidal zone is home to mussels and rock weed. This low intertidal zone, uncovered only when the ocean deeply recedes during minus tides, supports the most diverse life forms. Sea urchins, starfish, abalone, and anemones flourish here, as do crabs, octopus, and chitons, those oval-shaped mollusks that date back to before the age of dinosaurs.

ture, and more attractive surroundings. At *deluxe*-priced accommodations, expect to spend $120 to $175 for a homey bed and breakfast or a double in a hotel or resort. You'll usually find spacious rooms, inviting lobbies and some choice outdoor additions such as patios, gardens, and pools. If you want to spend your time (and money) at the finest hotels—try an *ultra-deluxe* facility, which will include all the amenities and cost over $175.

For information on the full range of accommodations available in the Santa Barbara area, there are two centralized reservation agencies. One is **Coastal Escapes Accommodations**. ~ 5320 Carpinteria Avenue, Carpinteria; 800-292-2222; www.coastalescapes.com. **Santa Barbara Hotspots** can also give information on prices and availability. ~ 36 State Street; 805-564-1637, 800-793-7666; www.hotspotsusa.com. Since room rates in Santa Barbara fluctuate by season and day of the week, it's advisable to check ahead.

DINING

It seems as if the California coast has more restaurants than people. To establish a pattern for this parade of dining places, we've organized them according to location and cost. Restaurants listed offer lunch and dinner unless otherwise noted. Within a particular chapter, the restaurant listings are categorized geographically and each individual restaurant entry describes the establishment as budget, moderate, deluxe, or ultra-deluxe in price.

Dinner entrées at *budget* restaurants usually cost $9 or less. The ambience is informal-café style and the crowd is often a local one. *Moderate*-priced restaurants range between $9 and $18 at dinner and offer pleasant surroundings, a more varied menu, and a slower pace. *Deluxe* establishments tab their entrées from $18 to $25, featuring sophisticated cuisines, plush decor, and more personalized service. *Ultra-deluxe* dining rooms, where $25 will only get you started, are gourmet gathering places where cooking (one hopes) is a fine art form and service a way of life.

Breakfast and lunch menus vary less in price from restaurant to restaurant. Even deluxe kitchens usually offer light breakfasts and lunch sandwiches, placing them within a few dollars of their budget-minded competitors. These early meals can be a good time to test expensive restaurants.

CALENDAR OF LOCAL EVENTS

JANUARY The **Hang Gliding Festival** on New Year's day opens aviation to locals and visitors with demonstrations and lessons by Santa Barbara's premier "foot-launched flyers." The festival runs 12 noon to sunset at Elings Park, weather permitting.

FEBRUARY The city's biggest star-studded event is **Santa Barbara's International Film Festival**, drawing Hollywood's elite and film fanatics to the coast. Held in various theaters around the city.

MARCH If you've got an eye for Laelia and Odontoglossum visit Santa Barbara's **International Orchid Show,** featuring over 70 of the world's finest growers and thousands of their most-prized plants. Held at the Earl Warren Showgrounds every year around the spring equinox.

Let's go fly a kite! The **Shoreline Kite Festival** has been a Santa Barbara tradition for nearly two decades. Participants flock to Shoreline Park to compete in stunt flying and exquisite wind-borne decorations.

Stearns Wharf hosts the city's **Whale Festival**, where biologists and naturalists expose land-locked souls to the Pacific's largest inhabitants. Music, arts and crafts, and food top off the marine festivities at the end of State Street.

APRIL Few know that **Earth Day** was launched in Santa Barbara following the devastating oil spill of 1969 that decimated marine life and stained the picturesque coastline. Today the annual celebration is held on the Sunday closest to April 22.

Food, music, and crafts fill the festivities at the **Jewish Festival** at Oak Park in Santa Barbara.

Presidio Days celebrates the original Spanish fort's conception in 1782 on Saint Barbara's birthday, April 21. Festivities culminate when Chumash and Spanish descendants ring the bells of the Presidio's tower.

On the third weekend of April local wineries draw connoisseurs and the curious alike to the **Santa Barbara County Vintners' Festival**. Held throughout the vine-striped Santa Ynez Valley (tickets must be purchased in advance).

The **Santa Barbara Fair and Expo** brings games, carnival rides, live music, and a full petting zoo to Earl Warren Showgrounds at the end of April.

MAY **Cinco de Mayo**, celebrating Mexico's defeat of French forces at the town of Puebla, is a multicultural celebration that spreads throughout Santa Barbara with music, food, and dance.

Santa Barbara takes on an Italian flavor during **Memorial Day Weekend** for the *we Maddonnari* celebration. Hundreds of chalk paintings color the Mission Courtyard, while across the street an Italian market features authentic foods and entertainment.

Mid-Summer Madness

Summer Solstice is one of Santa Barbara's wackiest events of the summer. Created by local street artists, this colorful festival has evolved into the biggest yearly celebration in town. Odd motorless floats and even weirder people march down State Street to Alameda Park, where dancing, crafts, food, and a beer-garden keep the party rocking and rolling. A children's area features storytellers, musicians, jugglers, and face-painters. This fun-filled celebration takes place at high noon on the Saturday closest to June 21. ~ www.solsticeparade.com.

JUNE   Santa Barbara takes canine fashion very seriously. The **Big Dog Parade and Canine Festival** on State Street (at Chase Palm Park) allows pooches to put on their best and strut their stuff for a handful of prizes.

The **Jose Cuervo Volleyball Tournament** at East Beach in Santa Barbara lures the tan and buff for some surf, sand, and sport.

Catch a whiff of Lompoc at the **Lompoc Flower Festival**, where the vibrant colors of spring and summer envelope the valley on floats, in gardens, and at one of California's best flower shows.

JULY   Hawaii meets the mainland coast for the **California Outrigger Championships** as state teams compete just off Leadbetter Beach.

The **French Festival** at Oak Park in Santa Barbara marks Bastille Day with food, wine, entertainment, and free admission. As the largest French celebration west of the Mississippi, it never disappoints.

Santa Barbara's Big Fat—**Greek Festival** kicks off in late July. A favorite of locals, the celebration fills Oak Park with dancing and shish kebab.

The sleepy shoreline explodes with **Santa Barbara's Independence Day Celebration.** Around 9 p.m. thousands flock to the waterfront for fireworks, music, and a beach party.

Equine and flora fanatics will find paradise at **Santa Barbara's National Horse and Flower Show.** For two weeks Earl Warren Showgrounds is graced with some of the west's finest breeds of horses and local blossoms.

Santa Barbara County Fair brings this long-standing California tradition to the central coast. Livestock auctions, food, and entertainment makes for a hootin' good time. Held at the County Fairgrounds in Santa Maria.

AUGUST   The Santa Ynez Valley kicks off August with the **Old Mission Santa Inés Fiesta,** celebrating the diverse Latino and Chumash cultures with food, dance, and festivities.

Festa Italiana is one of the area's premier ethnic celebrations. Pasta, pizza, *e tutti le cose Italiane* fill Oak Park with the smells of classic Italy.

Fiesta or "**Old Spanish Days**" is the soul of Santa Barbara. Launched in 1924, the five-day festival brings the entire city together in the spirit of the old *ranchos*. Festivities held throughout the city include the largest equestrian parade in the States, a rodeo, and a whole heap of food, music, and arts.

SEPTEMBER   You might not expect to find the spirit of Denmark in the heart of California but it's there. Every year in the middle of

September the Dane-inspired town of Solvang erupts with beer, food, and dancing for **Danish Days**.

The **Annual Taste of the Town** is a week-long feast of more than 50 of the region's finest restaurants and wineries. Tickets must be purchased in advance for the afternoon events held at Riviera Research Park Gardens.

Dixie, jazz, and blues fill the salt air of Santa Barbara for the **International Jazz Festival**. The biennial festival boasts some of the world's premier musicians for a weekend of fantastic music and entertainment; held throughout Santa Barbara.

OCTOBER The Santa Barbara Museum of Natural History holds an annual **Art-walk** featuring dozens of artists who display their work along the museum grounds. The weekend event benefits the museum.

The coast's greenest pit-stop is Carpinteria's **California Avocado Festival**. To honor the fruit, chefs, avocado nuts, and guac-fanatics roll out some of the strangest dishes imaginable—including avocado ice cream and the world's largest bowl of guacamole.

With their grapes plump and ripe the vintners of the Santa Ynez Valley hold a **Celebration of Harvest** in early October. The Saturday festivities (usually the second Saturday of the month) feature local wines as well as food from the valley's favorite restaurants.

The **Goleta Lemon Festival** is a unique celebration of the sour. Lemon pie contests, lemonade stands, food, arts, and entertainment make for a wild citrus party.

Every other year, in early October, the blue skies of Santa Barbara echo with jet engines and daredevil prop-planes for the **Santa Barbara Air Fair** at the city's Municipal Airport.

NOVEMBER Break out the cross-trainers and head for Leadbetter Beach

to participate in the Santa Barbara News-Press' **Half-Marathon and Cally's 5K Fun Run and Walk.**

DECEMBER   Although it may be 75 degrees outdoors Santa Barbara begins to feel a lot like Christmas when State Street holds the **Downtown Holiday Parade.** Shops remain open late into the night for parade-goers to have a chance to finish their holiday shopping.

The **Folk and Tribal Arts Marketplace** is a three-day event in early December that brings crafts from every corner of the planet to the Santa Barbara Museum of Natural History.

The **Parade of Lights** is one of Santa Barbara's favorite winter celebrations. From Stearns Wharf you can watch boats cruise the waterfront dressed up in bright lights and festive decorations.

Every year Solvang hangs their wreaths and decks the town in holiday spirit for **Winterfest.** The month-long celebration culminates with the lighting of the town's

Christmas tree and continues with a parade, pageant, and a lot of Danish pastries.

The **Santa Barbara Symphony** ushers in the New Year with a raucous sing-along concert of pop and Broadway hits.

OUTDOOR ACTIVITIES

This stretch of the Central Coast epitomizes California's natural beauty and offers year-round outdoor fun. The mild, sunny Mediterranean climate almost guarantees perfect conditions for active visitors. With its rolling, oak-studded hills and long, sandy beaches, Santa Barbara presents a wide variety of outdoor adventures, from surfing and whale watching to hiking and horseback riding.

Fishing

Because of its location along the Central Coast, both cold-water and warm-water fishing is possible in Santa Barbara. You'll find a number of experienced charter companies to take you out to prime fishing areas.

Sea Landing offers half-, three-quarter, and full-day cruises. Look to catch calico bass, red snapper, barracuda, and an occasional tuna. ~ 301 West Cabrillo Boulevard, Santa Barbara; 805-963-3564. **Patriot Sportfishing** specializes in deep-sea and rock fishing and targets salmon and albacore seasonally. ~ Pier 3, Avila Beach; 805-595-7200; www.patriotsportfishing.com. **Virge's Sportfishing** books three-quarter-day charters for

Ocean Safety

For swimming, surfing, and skindiving, few places match California's coastline. Many water lovers, however, never realize how destructive the sea can be. Particularly in California, where waves can reach

significant heights and currents often flow unobstructed, the ocean is sometimes as treacherous as it is spectacular. Unfortunately, people drown every year while others are dragged from the surf with serious injuries, and countless numbers sustain minor cuts and bruises. These accidents can be avoided if you relate to the Pacific with a respect for its magnificent power. All you have to do is heed two simple guidelines. First, never turn your back on the sea. Waves come in sets: one group may be small and quite harmless, but the next set could be large enough to sweep you out to sea. And second, never swim alone.

rock cod (in the fall) and overnight charters for albacore (from July to December). They also offer multiday trips from November to June. ~ 1215 Embarcadero, Morro Bay; 805-772-1222; www.virges.com.

If you'd rather drop a line from Stearns Wharf, **Angel's Bait & Tackle** rents poles and crab traps. No license necessary. ~ Stearns Wharf, Santa Barbara; 805-965-1333.

Whale Watching

If you're in the mood for a whale-watching excursion, take your pick from numerous companies. You can also opt for either of two whale-watching seasons. From January through May, you'll see California gray whales on their northern migration. The second season, from June to September, brings blue and humpback whales to the Channel Islands.

Contact **Channel Island Sportfishing** for tours from January through March. ~ 4151 South Victoria Avenue, Oxnard; 805-985-8511; www.sportfishingreport.com. For excursions in both seasons, call **Captain Don's**. From February through May, Captain Don's sails along the Santa Barbara coast on a 90-foot boat looking for gray whales around the Channel Islands. You're bound to see a sea lion, otter, or dolphin on the harbor cruise. ~ Stearns Wharf, Santa Barbara; 805-969-5217; www.captdon.com. **Sea Landing** will take you whale watching from December through October on the 75-foot *Condor Express*. ~ 301 West Cabrillo Boulevard, Santa Barbara; 805-963-3564; www.condor cruises.com. **Patriot Sportfishing** operates whale-watching tours from the end of December through April. The three-hour trips go in search of the California gray whale. ~ Pier 3, Avila Beach; 805-595-7200; www.patriotsport fishing.com.

Kayaking

Sea kayaking is excellent along the Central Coast and out to the Channel Islands. Many outfits offer tours, rentals, and lessons.

You can rent a kayak or arrange instructional paddling trips to the sea caves of Santa Cruz Island with **Aquasports**. ~ 111 Verona Avenue, Goleta; 805-968-7231, 800-773-2309; www.islandkayaking.com. **Adventours Outdoor Excursions, Inc.** can arrange trips combining kayaking with other outdoor activities such as camping, hiking, biking, and backpacking. ~ P.O. Box 215, Santa Barbara, CA 93102; 805-898-9569; www.adventours.com.

Diving

For those more interested in watching fish, several companies charter dive boats and also offer scuba diving rentals and lessons. The waters around the Channel Islands provide some of the world's best diving spots. In Santa Barbara, call **Anacapa Dive Center** for scuba instruction, rentals, and trips to the Channel Islands. ~ 22 Anacapa Street, Santa Barbara; 805-963-8917; www.anacapadivecenter.com. Dive charters to local waters and the Channel Islands are arranged by **Sea Landing**. They offer one-day open-water trips as well as two-, three-, and

five-day charters. ~ 301 West Cabrillo Boulevard, Santa
Barbara; 805-963-3564; www.truthaquatics.com.

Surfing

There's good surfing all along the Central Coast. Catch
a wave with surfboard rentals from the following enter-
prises.

The **Santa Barbara Adventure Company** will not
only teach you how to surf, they will take you kayaking
along the coast and over to the Channel Islands, or guide
you on a mountain biking adventure. They rent all the
gear and have professional guides for every activity. ~
P.O. Box 208, Santa Barbara, CA 93102; 805-452-1942,

Sovereigns of the Sea

Few animals inspire the sense of myth and magic associated with
the marine mammals of California's coastline. Foremost are
whales, dolphins, and porpoises, members of the unique cetacean
order that left the land 30 million years ago for the alien world
of the sea. Some dolphins and
porpoises range far offshore
and require boat tours for
viewing, but oftentimes
you can sit on the beach
and watch them frolic in
the waves, almost within
arm's reach. One of the region's
most common cetacean, the gray whale visits the coast in late
winter, early spring. Migrating 12,000 miles every year between
the Bering Sea and the Baja peninsula, the California gray whale
cruises the shoreline, offering marvelous shows when it breaches,
tail slashing and swishing. Measuring 50 feet and weighing 40 tons,
these distinguished animals can live to 50 years of age and com-
municate with sophisticated signaling systems.

888-596-6687; www.sbadventureco.com. In Goleta, **Surf Country** rents boards and offers lessons. ~ 5668 Calle Real, Goleta; 805-683-4450. **Ventura Surf Shop** rents surfboards and wetsuits. ~ 88 East Thompson Boulevard, Ventura; 805-643-1062.

Boating

The Central Coast and the Channel Islands are prime areas for boating. You can rent your own boat or go on one of the various cruises and charters offered.

To sail the Pacific, visit the Channel Islands, watch whales, or take a romantic sunset champagne cruise, contact **Santa Barbara Sailing Center** for boat rentals and charters. They also offer a variety of lessons. ~ The Breakwater, Santa Barbara; 805-962-2826, 800-350-9090; www.sbsail.com. **Sea Landing** offers cruises and charters. Sunset dinner trips are a specialty. ~ 301 West Cabrillo Boulevard, Santa Barbara; 805-963-3564. In summer **Captain Don's** has sunset and dinner cruises as well as sight-seeing tours. ~ Stearns Wharf, Santa Barbara; 805-969-5217; www.capt dons.com. In Ventura, **Pacific Sailing** provides sailboat charters and instruction. ~ 1583 Spinnaker Drive, Dock D-9, Ventura Harbor; 805-658-6508; www.pacsail.com.

Golf

Golf enthusiasts will enjoy the weather as well as the courses along the Central Coast. (Courses have 18 holes unless otherwise stated.)

Riders on the Storm

Along the curving shoreline of Santa Barbara, waves, born thousands of miles to the north and south, approach the shallow reefs, sandbars, and kelp forests to produce the breathtaking medium for one of California's most famous sports—surfing. The hundred-mile stretch of jagged cliffs, silky beaches, and rolling ranchlands from Oxnard to Buellton are probably best known as the priceless and protected havens for these elite watermen and women.

Just south of Santa Barbara, as Route 101 swings back toward the sea, lies one of California's notorious surf breaks—Rincon. This long, thin beach is a popular summer getaway for locals and tourists but sees little swell during the hotter months; it is not until winter, as massive storms gather around the Arctic Circle, that the break featured in such cult classics as *Endless Summer* begins to breathe. Mammoth waves curve around this perfect point break to produce some of the most awe-inspiring rides. Although these waves may appear gorgeous, they pack a serious punch, sometimes building to 20 feet or more.

Santa Barbara Golf Club's course is dotted with oaks, pines, and sycamores. ~ Las Positas Road and McCaw Avenue, Santa Barbara; 805-687-7087. The executive nine-hole **Twin Lakes Golf Course** meanders around two lakes. ~ 6034 Hollister Avenue, Goleta; 805-964-1414. Two miles north of Twin Lakes is **Sandpiper Golf Course**, a championship course right on the ocean. ~ 7925 Hollister Avenue, Goleta; 805-968-1541; www.sandpipergolf.com. A creek winds through the nine-hole **Ocean Meadows Golf Course**, which is a relatively flat playing field. ~ 6925 Whittier Drive, Goleta; 805-968-6814; www.oceanmeadowsgolf.com.

The **River Ridge Golf Club** is a links-style course with an island green on the 14th hole. ~ 2401 West Vineyard Avenue, Oxnard; 805-983-4653; www.river

ridge-golfclub.com. A flat course, **Olivas Park** comes complete with driving range and putting green. ~ 3750 Olivas Park Drive, Ventura; 805-642-4303.

A favorite destination for Hollywood duffers, the **Ojai Valley Inn & Spa** features a rolling course high in the hills. ~ 905 Country Club Road, Ojai; 805-646-2420; www.ojairesort.com. The course at **Rancho San Marcos** wanders past traces of the 19th-century San Marcos stage coach trail. ~ 4600 Route 154, Santa Ynez; 805-683-6334. **La Purísima**'s course traverses over 300 acres of oak-studded hills in the heart of Santa Barbara's wine country. ~ 3455 Route 246, Lompoc; 805-735-8395; www.lapurisimagolf.com.

Tennis

Tennis, anyone? This area offers a number of opportunities for tennis fiends. **Moranda Park Tennis Complex** has eight lighted courts situated in a beautiful park setting. Equipment rentals available. ~ 200 Moranda Parkway, Port Hueneme; 805-986-3587. **Santa Barbara Municipal Courts** features four facilities with a total of 32 courts; 14 are lighted. Bring your own equipment. Fee. ~ 1414 Park Place; 805-564-5517.

Horseback Riding

With its varied terrain and ocean-view vistas, the Central Coast offers a dramatic backdrop for equestrian pursuits.

Circle Bar B Stables takes riders on a one-and-a-half-hour trip through a canyon, past waterfalls, and then up to a vista point overlooking the Channel Islands. A half-day lunch ride is also available. Reservations are required. ~ 1800 Refugio Road, Goleta; 805-968-3901; www.cir clebarb.com.

Biking

Biking the Central Coast can be a rewarding experience. The coastal route, however, presents problems in populated areas, especially during rush hour.

Santa Barbara is chock-full of beautiful bike paths and trails. Two notable beach excursions are the **Atascadero Recreation Trail**, which starts at the corner of Encore Drive and Modoc Road and ends over seven miles later at Goleta Beach, and **Cabrillo Bikeway**, which takes you from Andree Clark Bird Refuge to Leadbetter Beach. Also, the University of California—Santa Barbara has many bike paths through the campus grounds and into Isla Vista.

Up the coast, a stunning, three-mile bike path links El Capitan and Refugio state beaches.

The town of **Ventura** offers an interesting bicycle tour through the historical section of town with a visit to the county historical museum and mission. Another bike tour of note, off Harbor Boulevard, leads to the Channel Islands National Park Visitors Center. The **Ventura River Trail** (6 miles) is an asphalt trail featuring locally designed sculptures and links to coastal, mountain, and downtown trails. A bike map of Ventura County is available at the **Ventura Visitors Bureau**. ~ 89

South California Street #C, Ventura; 805-648-2075; www.goventura.org.

Inland, you'll catch panoramic vistas along the 16.5-mile **Ojai Valley Trail**, which runs from Ojai to the ocean. **BIKE RENTALS AND TOURS** **Adventours Outdoor Excursions, Inc.** offers bike tours to the Santa Ynez Mountains, the Santa Ynez Valley wine country, and the Santa Barbara coast. ~ P.O. Box 215, Santa Barbara, CA 93102; 805-898-9569; www.adventours.com.

Wheel Fun Rentals rents tandems, three-wheelers, and mountain bikes. ~ 22 State Street, Santa Barbara; 805-966-2282. Rent beach cruisers or hybrid bikes from **Big Gear Bike Gear**. ~ 324 State Street, Santa Barbara; 805-962-5962. **Bicycles of Ojai** also offers rentals. Closed Sunday. ~ 108 Cañada Avenue, Ojai; 805-646-7736.

Hiking

What distinguishes Santa Barbara from most of California's coastal communities is the magnificent Santa Ynez mountain range, which forms a backdrop to the city and provides excellent hiking terrain.

A red steel gate marks the beginning of **Romero Canyon Trail** (7 miles) on Bella Vista Road in Santa Barbara. After joining a fire road at the 2350-foot elevation, the trail follows a stream shaded by oak, sycamore, and bay trees. From here you can keep climbing or return via the right fork, a fire road that offers an easier but longer return trip.

San Ysidro Trail (1.2 miles) begins at Park Lane and Mountain Drive in Santa Barbara, follows a stream dotted with pools and waterfalls, then climbs to the top of Camino Cielo ridge. For a different loop back, it's only a short walk to Cold Springs Trail.

Also located in the Santa Ynez Mountains is **Rattlesnake Canyon Trail** (1.75 miles). Beginning near Skofield Park, the trail follows Mission Creek, along which an aqueduct was built in the early 19th century. Portions of the waterway can still be seen. This pleasant trail offers shaded pools and meadows.

Cold Springs Trail, East Fork (4.5 miles) heads east from Mountain Drive in Santa Barbara. The trail takes you through a canyon covered with alder and along a creek punctuated by pools and waterfalls. It continues up into Hot Springs Canyon and crosses the flank of Montecito Peak.

Cold Springs Trail, West Fork (5 miles) leads off the better known East Fork. It climbs and descends along the left side of a lushly vegetated canyon before arriving at an open valley.

Tunnel Trail (2.9 miles) is named for the turn-of-the-20th-century tunnel through the mountains that brought fresh water to Santa Barbara. The trail begins at the end of Tunnel Road in Santa Barbara and passes through various sandstone formations and crosses a creek before arriving at Mission Falls.

Hiking trail in Goleta.

San Antonio Creek Trail (1.7 miles), an easy hike along a creek bed, starts from the far end of Tucker's Grove County Park in Goleta. In the morning or late afternoon you'll often catch glimpses of deer foraging in the woods.

Thirty-five miles of coastline stretches from Stearns Wharf in Santa Barbara to Gaviota State Beach. There are hiking opportunities galore along the entire span.

Summerland Trail (1-mile loop), starting at Lookout Park in Summerland, takes you along Summerland Beach, past tiny coves, then along Montecito's coastline to the beach fronting the Four Seasons Biltmore Hotel.

Goleta Beach Trail (2 miles) begins at Goleta Beach County Park in Goleta and curves past tidepools and sand dunes en route to Goleta Point. Beyond the dunes is Devereux Slough, a reserve populated by egrets, herons, plovers, and sandpipers. The hike also passes the Ellwood Oil Field, where a Japanese submarine fired shots at the mainland United States during World War II.

TRANSPORTATION

Car

As it proceeds north from the Los Angeles area, coastal highway **Route 1** weaves in and out from **Route 101**. The two highways join in Oxnard and continue as a single roadway, passing through Ventura, Carpinteria, and Summerland on the way to Santa Barbara. Goleta and Lompoc lie north of Santa Barbara along this combined route. At Ventura, **Route 33** meanders up into the hills on its way to Ojai. Just north of Santa Barbara, **Route 154** winds its way over the San Marcos Pass to Santa Ynez.

Air

Santa Barbara has a small airport serving the Central Coast. Airlines that stop at the **Santa Barbara Municipal Airport** include America West Express, American Eagle, Delta Connection, Horizon Air, and United Express. ~ 805-967-7111; www.flysba.com.

The **Santa Barbara Airbus** can be scheduled to meet arrivals at the airport; it otherwise goes to Carpinteria, Goleta, and downtown Santa Barbara, as well as Los Angeles International Airport. ~ 805-964-7759, 800-423-1618; www. sbairbus.com. For the disabled, call **Easy Lift Transportation.** ~ 805-681-1181.

Train

For those who want spectacular views of the coastline, try **Amtrak**'s "Coast Starlight" connecting Santa Barbara and Northern California and the "Pacific Surfliner," servicing the south coast. Both train lines hug the shoreline, providing rare views of the Central Coast's cliffs, headlands, and untracked beaches. The main Amtrak station is in Santa Barbara (209 State Street) with a substation in Goleta (north end of La Patera Lane). ~ 800-872-7245; www.amtrak.com.

Car Rentals

At the airport in Santa Barbara try **Avis Rent A Car** (800-331-1212), **Budget Rent A Car** (800-527-0700), **Hertz Rent A Car** (800-654-3131), or **National Car Rental** (800-227-7368). Agencies located outside the airport with free pick-up include **Enterprise Rent A Car** (800-325-8007).

In downtown Santa Barbara look for **Avis Rent A Car** (34 East Montecito Street; 805-965-1079) and **Hertz Rent A Car** (633 East Cabrillo Boulevard; 805-962-5305).

Public Transit

Although mass transit is a bit of a joke in Southern California Santa Barbara's bus system is actually a decent and efficient way to trek around town. The **Santa Barbara Metropolitan Transit** stops in Summerland, Carpinteria, Santa Barbara, Goleta, and Isla Vista. The **Downtown-Waterfront Shuttle**, also operated by MTD, is a popular open-air bus running between State Street and Stearns Wharf. ~ Carrillo and Chapala streets; 805-683-3702; www.sbmtd.gov.

2.

Downtown
Santa Barbara

Relaxed in feel and lovely to look at, downtown Santa Barbara feels more like a small European city than a California beach town. Pulsating and vital, with buildings of sparklingly white stucco and red-tiled roofs, this is where locals and visitors alike come to eat, party, and shop. Since the 1800s State Street had been a four-lane arterial road, but in the 1990s—in the interest of making downtown more walkable and attractive—the road was reduced to two lanes, the sidewalk was widened and bricked, and a bike path added. Today al fresco diners sip designer lattes and local wines while shaded by giant primary-colored umbrellas and such flowering trees as jacaranda and coral. Art galleries, antique shops, and boutiques have replaced the more practical and mundane businesses of the 1950s and '60s. Intriguing pieces of sculpture spill out of the galleries onto the street and into courtyards. Creative one-of-a-kind wrought iron signs hang outside specialty shops and restaurants. Buildings and fountains are adorned with decorative tile accents, while in cozy Spanish-style courtyards, with spewing fountains and dazzling

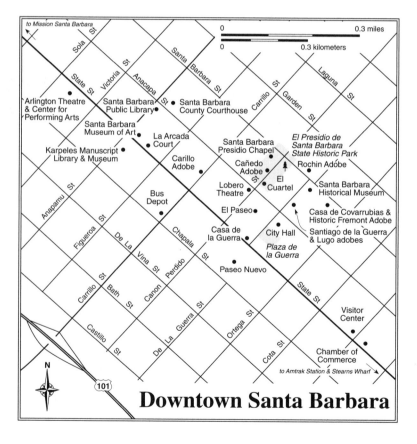

Downtown Santa Barbara

pink and red geraniums, people gather at outdoor

cafés or poke around upscale shops. Bordering State

Street to the northeast is where the town began and

where the remaining historical structures have been

lovingly preserved and renovated. With its distinc-

tive European-style architecture, and trees, flowers,

and temperatures that mimic the Mediterranean, it's

little wonder that Santa Barbara is often referred to

as California's Riviera.

SIGHTS

Santa Barbara is one of the few places in America where you can stroll by a building constructed in the early 1800s and not even notice it. Today the bustling beach city has grown well beyond the original footprint of early Santa Barbara; but tucked amid high-price shops and popular restaurants are the remains of early California, when the coast was ideal for ranching, not surfing.

History Between Plates

The Santa Barbara–Mediterranean facade that lures tourists to the beach city is thanks to California's greatest curse. By the mid-1920s Santa Barbara had become a favorite vacation destination for the rich and famous. The town had extravagant hotels, a perfect climate, miles of beach and was quickly losing its identity.

Santa Barbara citizens watched their secluded paradise submit to the uniform of American architecture, leaving long rows of bland buildings throughout the city. Some locals tried to launch a transformation in the city's style to rebuild buildings in Spanish adobe and red-tiled roofs, as it appears today, but failed to overcome the financial and bureaucratic opposition. Then, on June 29, 1925, a massive earthquake put Santa Barbara's overhaul into immediate motion. The earthquake, and two devastating aftershocks, destroyed most of the downtown. The remodeling of Santa Barbara into the breathtaking Spanish-style city it is today, though it took decades to accomplish, is, in part, thanks to California's most notorious feature.

Veering off the artery of downtown State Street, you will encounter two centuries of history. Everything from the old Spanish mission, presidio, and early adobe houses to the first influences of the American pioneers rests within a six-block radius of the modern heart of Santa Barbara. From the outside many of these historic buildings are identifiable only by weatherworn signs, chipped adobe walls, and roof tiles that have aged from red to rust. Although these sights seem to slip into the Spanish-style architecture of the city without notice, they represent the earthy foundation for the seaside city and are well worth a visit.

The city's grandest building, the **Santa Barbara County Courthouse**, is a U-shaped Spanish Moorish "palace" that covers almost three sides of a city block. The interior is a masterwork of beamed ceilings, arched corridors, and *palacio* tile floors. On the second floor of this 1929 courthouse are murals depicting California history. The highlight of every visit is the sweeping view of Santa Barbara at the top of the clock tower, one of Santa Barbara's highest points. From the Santa Ynez Mountains down to the ocean, all that meets the eye are palm trees and red-tiled roofs. No tours on Sunday. ~ 1100 block of Anacapa Street; 805-962-6464, fax 805-967-4104.

Santa Barbara County Courthouse.

Two blocks down from the courthouse is the **Carrillo Adobe**, an 1826 vintage home built by a Massachusetts settler, Daniel Hill, for his Spanish bride. The house is closed to the public but can be viewed from the street. ~ 11 East Carrillo Street.

Along State Street many stores occupy antique buildings. **El Paseo**, built in 1924, represents the first shopping mall west of the Mississippi. With Spanish tile, gleaming white stucco, graceful archways, gurgling fountains, and flowering courtyards, El Paseo was the first project built in the Spanish style that became the city's unique architectural character. Today, you can wander through from Anacapa Street to State, passing through narrow, white-washed adobe corridors and intimate, sun-baked courtyards. Although much of this shopping center has been converted to office space, there are a few restaurants and shops hidden within its maze. This is the perfect place to enjoy a picnic lunch or a café au lait in an atmosphere of blissful tranquility. ~ 812 State Street.

Possibly the inspiration for Santa Barbara's architectural motif was **Casa de la Guerra**, a splendid house built in 1818 for the commander of the Santa Barbara Presidio and described by Richard Henry Dana in his classic book *Two Years Before the Mast*. The building was purchased from the De la Guerra family by Bernard Hoffman, an engineer from the East Coast and the driving force behind Santa Barbara's Spanish remodeling. In 1924, drawing inspiration from the house's architecture, Hoffman began building the El Paseo shopping mall next door. Closed Monday through Wednesday. Admission. ~ 15 East de la Guerra Street; 805-965-0093; www.sbthp.org, e-mail info@sbthp.org.

Across the street rests **Plaza de la Guerra**, a palm-fringed park where the first city hall stood in 1875. Nearby, another series of historic structures have been converted into a warren of shops and offices. In the center of the mall is Presidio Gardens, a tranquil park with a carp pond and elephant-shaped fountains that spray water through their trunks. ~ On De la Guerra Street between Anacapa and Garden streets.

The **Santiago de la Guerra Adobe** and the **Lugo Adobe**, set in a charming courtyard, are other 19th-century homes that have been converted to private use. ~ 114 East de la Guerra Street.

The **Santa Barbara Historical Museum** certainly looks its part. Set in an adobe building with tile roof and wrought iron window bars, the facility sits behind heavy wooden doors. Within are fine art displays and a series

Santa Barbara Historical Museum.

depicting the Spanish, Mexican, and early American periods of Santa Barbara's history. There is a pleasant courtyard in back with a fountain and shade trees, a perfect place for a sightseer's siesta. Closed Monday. ~ 136 East de la Guerra Street; 805-966-1601, fax 805-966-1603; www.santabarbaramuseum.com.

Most places in town are a little too neatly refurbished to provide a dusty sense of history. However, **Casa de Covarrubias**, an L-shaped house, along with the adjacent **Historic Fremont Adobe**, are sufficiently wind blasted to evoke the early 19th century. The former structure, dating to 1817, is said to be the site of the last Mexican assembly in 1846; the latter became headquarters for Colonel John C. Fremont after Americans captured the town later that year. ~ 715 North Santa Barbara Street.

It's a few steps over to **El Presidio de Santa Barbara State Historic Park**, which occupies both sides of the street and incorporates some of the city's earliest buildings. Founded in 1782, the Presidio was one of four military fortresses built by the Spanish in California. Providing a safe haven for white settlers and missionaries, it also served as a seat of government and center of Western culture. Today only two original buildings survive. **El Cuartel**, the guards' house, served as the soldiers' quarters. The **Cañedo Adobe**, also built as a military residence, is now the offices of the Santa Barbara Trust for Historic Preservation. Most interesting of all is the **Santa Barbara Presidio Chapel**, which re-creates an early Spanish church in its full array of colors. Compared to the plain exterior, the interior is a jolt to the eye. Everything is done in red and yellow ocher and dark blue. The altar is painted to simulate a great cathedral. Drapes and columns, difficult to obtain during Spanish days, have been drawn onto the walls. Even the altar railing is painted to imitate colored marble. The latest addition to the historic park is the 1856 **Rochin Adobe** (820 Santa Barbara Street). Admission. ⌐ 123 East Cañon Perdido Street; 805-966-9719; www.sbthp.org, e-mail info@sbthp.org.

The **Lobero Theatre**, constructed in 1924, is a three-tiered design that ascends to a 70-foot-high stage house. The original Lobero Theatre, named for its founder, an Italian immigrant, Jose Lobero, dates back to 1873, Santa Barbara's first theater. Today the Lobero presents a variety of performing arts. Call Monday through Saturday for tickets. ⌐ 33 East

Lobero Theatre office.

Cañon Perdido Street; 805-963-0761, fax 805-963-8752; www.lobero.com.

Santa Barbara Museum of Art adds a local flair to its collection of American and European paintings and photography, Asian art, and classical sculpture. Housed in a Spanish adobe, the museum highlights California's rugged cowboy past, with works by local artists that focus on Santa Barbara's early ranching existence. Closed Monday. Admission. ~ 1130 State Street; 805-963-4364, fax 805-966-6840; www.sbmuseart.org.

Even if you're not a history buff or literary aficionado, it's hard not to be seduced by **Karpeles Manuscript Library and Museum**. Where else can you see an original stone copy of the Declaration of Independence, a replica of the globe used by Columbus, handwritten scores by a dozen leading composers, and the computer guidance system used on the first Apollo lander flight to the moon. Besides their permanent collection, there are special exhibits covering everything from vaccination to early baseball, and it can all be enjoyed free of charge. ~ 21 West Anapamu Street; 805-962-5322; www.rain.org/~karpeles/sb.html.

At the **Arlington Theatre & Center for Performing Arts**, a Spanish courtyard with fountains leads through the lobby into the auditorium, where the walls are painted with murals depicting a Spanish town. Overhead a dark blue concave ceiling twinkles with hundreds of tiny lights. One of the few remaining picture palaces built in the 1920s, the mission revival style Arlington Theatre is a gem. In Hollywood's heyday, Santa Barbara was a favorite spot to preview new movies, and stars came to the Arlington to promote their latest film. Today the Arlington has been beautifully restored and remains a one-screen theater that still features first-run Hollywood blockbusters, as well as live performances. ~ 1317 State Street; 805-963-4408.

LODGING

Inn of the Spanish Garden
915 Garden Street
805-564-4700, 866-564-4700, fax 805-564-4701
www.spanishgardeninn.com, e-mail info@spanishgardeninn.com
23 rooms
ULTRA-DELUXE

A lovely retreat just a few minutes walk from the center of downtown, Inn of the Spanish Garden is a boutique hotel at its best. Spacious rooms come with fireplaces, deep-water soaking tubs, French press coffee makers, and private balconies; towels and linens are by Frette. A complimentary continental breakfast, complete with espresso drinks, can be enjoyed in courtyards brimming with flowers and punctuated by gurgling fountains. Other amenities include a fitness center, a pool, in-room spa treatments, and a caring and efficient staff.

In-town Spas

Santa Barbara is almost always on the cutting edge of the latest trend, and downtown day spas are no exception. There are possibly more day spas per capita in downtown Santa Barbara than anywhere else in the country. And there's nothing like being massaged and pampered at one of them to improve everything from sore feet to a tension headache. **Avia Spa** combines Eastern philosophy with Western technology to give their customers the ultimate spa experience. ~ 350 Chapala Street, Suite 101 and 102; 805-730-7303; www.aviaspa.com. **Spa Medicus**, a skin care spa supervised by medical professionals, offers a broad spectrum of services from soothing, deep-pore cleansing facials to botox and collagen treatments. ~ 18 East Cañon Perdido Street; 805-966-4772. **Le Reve** puts an emphasis on relaxation with fountains, soft music, and aromatic scents accompanying facials, massages, and body treatments. ~ 1614 State Street; 805-564-2977; www.le-reve.com. **Qui Si Bella** takes inspiration from ancient Roman bath rituals with hydrotherapy tubs and a program for "The Renaissance Man," which includes something called an après golf treatment. ~ 3311 State Street; 805-682-0003.

Hotel Santa Barbara
533 State Street
805-957-9300, 800-549-9869, fax 805-962-2412
www.hotelsantabarbara.com, e-mail information@hotelsanta
   barbara.com
75 rooms
DELUXE

Located right on State Street, no hotel is more convenient to downtown than the Hotel Santa Barbara. The establishment is a perfect example of how a faded and shabby old downtown hotel can be transformed into a boutique property with some renovation and creative decorating. While the best vestiges of the hotel, like the Spanish tile staircase, remain, the rooms have all been updated and are bright and airy. Continental breakfast is included in the price of the room and coffee, tea, hot chocolate, and fresh fruit are available all day.

DINING

Wine Cask

813 Anacapa Street
805-966-9463
www.winecask.com, e-mail winecask@winecask.com
no lunch on weekends
ULTRA-DELUXE

One of the more romantic restaurants in Santa Barbara is the Wine Cask, where you can dine outside in a lovely courtyard or indoors under the colorful hand-painted ceiling mural that dates from the 1920s. Among the innovative entrées are seared peppercorn-crusted ahi and herb-crusted Colorado lamb loin, as well as chicken, beef, and pastas. Appetizers are equally creative and tempting. Don't forget to check out the wine list with more than 3500 vintages.

Joe's Café

536 State Street
805-966-4638
BUDGET TO DELUXE

Santa Barbara natives have been eating at Joe's Café since 1928. Crowds line the coal black bar, pile into the booths, and fill the tables. They come for a meat and potatoes lunch and dinner menu that stars prime rib. This is where you go for pork chops, steak, and French dip. The walls are loaded with mementos and faded photographs; softball trophies and deer antlers decorate the place; and the noise level is the same as the Indy 500. Paradise for slummers.

Sojourner Coffeehouse

134 East Cañon Perdido
805-965-7922
www.sojournercafe.com, e-mail sojo@sojournercafe.com
lunch, dinner and weekend brunch
BUDGET TO MODERATE

Hanging out in coffeehouses is my favorite avocation. There's no better spot in Santa Barbara than Sojourner Coffeehouse. Not only do they serve espresso and cappuccino, but lunch, dinner, and weekend brunch as well. Everyone seems to know everyone else in this easygoing café. They come to kibitz and enjoy the tostadas, rice and vegetable plates, and gourmet salads. The accent is vegetarian so expect daily specials like polenta cake royale, sweet tomato linguini, or garden Indian dhal.

La Fiesta

For five days in August, Santa Barbara is transformed from a laid-back beach town into a south-of-the-border street festival. Señoritas in brightly colored, ruffled dresses stroll with sombreroed partners, downtown stores are decorated with red, green, and white streamers, and strangers greet each other with cries of "Viva la Fiesta." For the past 80 years Santa Barbara has celebrated the period of its history when the city was under Spanish and Mexican influence with the **Old Spanish Days Fiesta**. What started out in 1924 as a modest affair has turned into a five-day extravaganza, including parades, barbecues, a rodeo, and Spanish-style entertainment. While the equestrian-dominated Fiesta Parade is impressive, don't miss the Children's Parade, where the local kids don traditional costumes and strut their stuff. ~ 805-962-8101; www.oldspanishdays-fiesta.org.

Esau's
403 State Street
805-965-4416
BUDGET

For truly prodigious breakfasts, locals know that nondescript Esau's is the place. Pancakes, omelettes, scrambles, and homemade hash are nicely prepared and served in generous portions. If there's a queue (usually the case on weekends), look for a stool at the counter.

The Palace Grill
8 East Cota Street
805-963-5000, fax 805-962-3200
www.palacegrill.com
MODERATE TO DELUXE

The graphics on the wall tell a story about the cuisine at The Palace Grill. Portrayed are jazz musicians, catfish, redfish, and scenes from New Orleans. The message is

Cajun, Creole, and Italian, and this lively, informal bistro is very good at delivering it. This restaurant prepares soft-shelled crab, blackened filet mignon, crawfish etouffee, jambalaya, pastas, and grilled steak. For dessert, Honey, we have Key lime pie and bread pudding.

Downey's

1305 State Street
805-966-5006, fax 805-966-5000
www.downeyssb.com
dinner only; closed Monday
ULTRA-DELUXE

Downey's, a small understated dining room, numbers among Santa Barbara's premier restaurants. The dozen tables here are set amid sage-colored walls lined with local artwork. The food is renowned: specializing in California cuisine, Downey's has a menu that changes daily. A typical evening's entrées are salmon with forest mushrooms, lamb loin with grilled eggplant and chiles, sea bass with artichokes, duck with fresh papaya chutney, and swordfish cooked over a mesquite grill. There is a good wine list featuring California vintages. Very highly recommended.

Bouchon Santa Barbara

9 West Victoria Street
805-730-1160, fax 805-564-2168
www.bouchonsantabarbara.com, e-mail info@bouchonsanta
    barbara.com
DELUXE

Dimly lit, with a soothingly muted color scheme, and good sound proofing, Bouchon Santa Barbara offers a romantic and peaceful dining experience whether eating inside or on the patio. The emphasis here is on using the freshest homegrown ingredients to produce creative dishes accompanied by carefully selected local wines. Pan-seared local halibut comes with beurre rouge, charred-tomato polenta cake, and braised artichoke hearts; the venison is from Santa Ynez Valley, the organic greens are grown locally, and the ice cream is McConnells, a Santa Barbara tradition for more than 50 years. The wait staff is well versed in the region's wines and encourage diners to choose the perfect one to accompany each course.

Roy
7 West Carrillo Street
805-966-5636
www.restaurantroy.com, e-mail roy@restaurantroy.com
dinner only
MODERATE

Every 45 days a different artist's work is hung on the walls of Roy, giving the restaurant a constantly changing look. They also have a Monday backgammon tournament and periodic live music, but its real draw is the food and the price. A welcome relief from à la carte menus with small portions and big prices, a fixed-price dinner comes with salad, soup, and nouveau American main courses, such as wild king salmon with fresh fruit salsa, local halibut in almond sauce, or fettuccine with prawns, all for a mere $20. So it's no surprise that there's a line to score a table on the weekends. It has a full bar and is open until midnight, making it a great place for after-theater dining.

Taiko
511 State Street
805-564-8875
BUDGET TO MODERATE

Asian starkness, Japanese graphic art, and jazz music gives Taiko a contemporary and sophisticated feel. Diners can start with a tasting of five different premium sakes, and continue in sampling mode by ordering the bento box, a potpourri of taste treats that vary daily but might

---

Public Art

Public art is not a new thing in downtown Santa Barbara. Though the art galleries of today display larger-than-life sculptures outside their stores, and the **Santa Barbara Museum of Art**'s temporary pieces of sculpture and murals adorn outside public areas, there are some permanent works that have been around for decades. *Fiesta*, a mural by Samuel Armstrong, has adorned the facade entry of the **Arlington Theatre** since 1931. ~ 1317 State Street. Around the corner on a **Von's Supermarket** wall, a six-panel, 224,640-individual-tiled mural by Joseph Knowels, completed in 1959, depicts the *History of Santa Barbara County*. ~ 34 West Victoria Street. And since 1981 a bronze statue of *Sacagawea* by Harry Jackson has stood in front of what is currently the **Washington Mutual** building. ~ 1330 State Street.

PICTURE-PERFECT
Breakfast spots

1. **Esau's, *p. 51***
2. **Tupelo Junction Café, *p. 58***
3. **Our Daily Bread, *p. 57***

include miso soup, a mixed green salad, spinach *ohitashi*, teriyaki chicken, scallop *kakiage* (tempura scallop and julienne vegetables), grilled salmon with *ponzu* sauce, and a California roll.

Olio E Limone
17 West Victoria Street
805-899-2699, fax 805-963-4858
no lunch on Sunday
DELUXE

The *piccolo* dining room at Olio E Limone is elegantly simple, with uncluttered neutral-colored walls and pristine white linens. On warm summer nights the patio is packed. As far as the food, forget the diet if you go to this Sicilian-owned restaurant. The dishes at this little slice of Italy include such hard to resist choices as roasted foie gras and grilled endive in a balsamic reduction sauce, beef tenderloin served over a potato tart with arugula, shaved parmesan, and truffle oil, and duck ravioli surrounded by a creamy porcini mushroom sauce. Desserts, like the pear-and-marzipan tart with warm caramel sauce, and eggless custard with fresh berries and fig balsamic sauce, are equally tempting.

Chinatown Original

Jimmie's Oriental Garden has been around since the days when it was the only Asian restaurant in town. Located in what was originally the city's Chinatown, the facade is typical of old-time Chinese restaurants, with tile, rounded windows, and a curved roofline. Inside, Chinese prints of bare-breasted women hang over red banquettes, and the food, such as *wor* wonton soup and almond-pressed duck, is traditional, tasty, and reasonably priced. This is a real local joint where regulars go to sip perfectly blended after-work cocktails and, on weekends, theatergoers gather after the show. No lunch on Sunday. Closed Monday. ~ 126 East Cañon Perdido Street; 805-962-7582, fax 805-965-3945. BUDGET TO MODERATE.

Cajun Kitchen Café
901 Chapala Street
805-965-1004, fax 805-965-8165
www.cajunkitchensb.com
breakfast and lunch
BUDGET TO MODERATE

In business for over 20 years, and with four locations around town, Cajun Kitchen Café is the only place I know of in Santa Barbara where you can get jambalaya topped with eggs for breakfast. The restaurant occupies the freestanding building that was for years the Jolly Tiger coffee shop. It still has a 1960s coffee shop feel, but with a Cajun twist, thanks to the photos of New Orleans covering the walls. The breakfast menu has a combination of American, Mexican, and Louisiana dishes, ranging from a breakfast burrito to eggs benedict to blackened catfish. For lunch, entrées include crawfish etouffee, file gumbo, and Po Boys, as well as the usual burgers and deli sandwiches for the less adventurous palate.

Café Buenos Aires

1316 State Street
805-963-0242, fax 805-963-0245
www.cafebuenosaires.com
MODERATE TO DELUXE

The Café Buenos Aires simply oozes atmosphere. Live Latin music echoes around the tiled patio while diners sip trendy martinis and South American cocktails such as caipirinhas, pisco sours, and mojitos. The food is an eclectic mix of Argentinean, Spanish, and Italian, including such specialties as Argentine-style spinach ravioli with prosciutto and mushrooms in a cream sauce, and free-range New York steak served alongside Argentine fries with garlic and *chimichurri porteno* sauce. The outside is loudly Latin so consider eating indoors for a quieter dining experience.

Our Daily Bread

831 Santa Barbara Street
805-966-3894, fax 805-966-6254
breakfast, lunch, and afternoon tea; closed Sunday
BUDGET

Our Daily Bread.

Nowhere beats Our Daily Bread for the freshest, tastiest bread in town. The baguettes are the best this side of Paris with a crispy crust and soft richly textured middle, and specialty breads run the gamut from New York Jewish rye to tomato-gorgonzola-walnut focaccia. The coffee drinks are a great accompaniment to the homemade scones, muffins, croissants, and pastries, and sandwiches are served on freshly baked focaccia, ciabatta, or multi-grain. This is one of the best places in town for a light breakfast, which can be enjoyed either in the delicious-smelling restaurant or at a streetside table.

dish
138 East Cañon Perdido
805-966-5365
www.eatdish.com
dinner only
DELUXE

Sparse and industrial, with burnt red walls, a distinctive white, waved ceiling, lots of gray steel, and glass- topped tables, dish is a trendy downtown restaurant that prepares gourmet Pacific Rim cuisine using organic produce. Specialties include grilled organic lamb loin, wild boar shank, slow-cooked *kung pao* short ribs, and duck, all with Asian touches. For appetizers there are more traditional offerings such as dim sum (Chinese dumplings). It's been reported that some of the entrées are skimpy, however, so if you're ravenous ask about the size of the portion before ordering.

Tupelo Junction Café
1212 State Street
805-899-3100, fax 805-899-3133
www.tupelojunction.com, e-mail info@tupelojunctioncafe.com
breakfast and lunch daily; dinner Wednesday through Sunday
BUDGET TO MODERATE

For a culinary trip to the South drop into the Tupelo Junction Café. Hardly the place for low-carb dieters or heart-smart devotees, the Tupelo specializes in rib-stick-

Unusual Bookstores

Considering that, according to the 2000 census, 79 percent of Santa Barbara County residents are high school graduates or higher, it's no wonder that the city has enough book lovers to support an intriguing mix of specialty bookstores. The **Book Den** has been the city's premier used bookstore for over 70 years. ~ 12 East Anapamu Street; 805-965-2844; www.book den.com. Next door the elegant **Sullivan Goss Book & Prints** antiquarian bookstore specializes in art books and prints. ~ 7 East Anapamu Street; 805-969-5112. **Lost Horizon Bookstore** appeals to artists and historians with books on the decorative arts, California history, Western Americana, and architecture. ~ 703 Anacapa Street; 805-962-4606. **Pacific Travelers Supply** is geared toward travelers, selling guidebooks, maps, and travel accessories. ~ 12 West Anapamu Street; 805-963-4438. The metaphysically minded should head to **Paradise Found** for books on everything from tarot card reading to meditation. ~ 17 East Anapamu Street; 805-564-3573; www.paradise-found.net.

ing, incredibly tasty Southern cooking at its best. The atmosphere is down-home Americana with fruit-crate labels as wall art, mason jars for sipping mimosas, and country-crock coffee mugs. For a positively sinful breakfast that transcends the ordinary, try the pumpkin-oatmeal waffles with caramelized bananas and candied pecans, crab cakes with potato hash, cinnamon-apple-and-ricotta *beignets*, or buttermilk biscuits smothered in sausage gravy.

Sage & Onion
34 East Ortega Street
805-963-1012, fax 805-963-8584
www.sageandonion.com, e-mail info@sageandonion.com
no lunch Saturday through Monday
DELUXE

At the Sage & Onion, creative food is served in a relaxing atmosphere. Decorated in muted colors with intimate lighting and a patio dining option, the restaurant offers up a tempting selection of starters and main courses. Begin appropriately with the toasted sage-and-onion biscuit with a warm poached egg before moving on to an apple-floured veal chop with kohlrabi gratin–malted pan gravy. Accompany the delicious food with a local wine and finish with a dessert soufflé. Yum!

Arigato Sushi
1225 State Street
805-965-6074, fax 805-730-9213
dinner only
DELUXE

Serving the best sushi that Santa Barbara has to offer, Arigato Sushi is very popular and does not accept reservations. But fear not: due to a pager system, you can shop State Street until you're called for your table. The sushi chefs are true artists and their creations superb. Try the gold shot (fresh local sea urchin, quail egg, *ponzu* sauce in a shot glass) or the Dungeness crab roll washed down with sake served in a bamboo cup. Cooked items,

HIDDEN

Booklover's Bistro

Tucked into a quiet courtyard in back of the Sullivan Goss bookstore, the **Arts & Letters Café** is a perfect place for a leisurely lunch. Linger over one of the creative salads, sandwiches, or main courses, such as roasted leg of lamb, artichoke-olive pesto and tomato jam on focaccia, or grilled Italian sausage with polenta and Roma tomato *fresca*, while sipping a local wine and you'll feel like you've been transported to Europe without having to spring for the plane fare. Lunch only. ~ 7 East Anapamu Street; 805-730-1463, fax 805-730-1462; www.sullivangoss.com, e-mail sales@sullivangoss.com. MODERATE.

such as scallop in a black sesame sauce and sautéed but-
terfish, are equally as delicious.

Rocks

801 State Street
805-884-1190, fax 805-564-4170
MODERATE

Rocks is a happening place on the corner of State
Street and the Paseo Nuevo shopping center. The food is
California-Asian and includes such mouth-watering specialties as roasted Chilean sea bass with orange butter
sauce and herb mashed potatoes, tuna carpaccio, and spicy
Korean-style ribs with fried rice. If you want to view the
action up close and personal, grab an outside table on the
street; to watch the action from above, sip your libation
with the in crowd on the second-floor balcony.

Los Arroyos

14 West Figueroa Street
805-962-5541, fax 805-962-2341
BUDGET TO MODERATE

Los Arroyos is a little gem of a downtown Mexican restaurant that made its reputation by serving tacos without parallel. Everything served here is unfailingly fresh and homemade, including the corn tortillas, which bear almost no resemblance to the pale-by-comparison store-bought variety. Salsas go from mild to four-alarm, and specialties include soft tacos with *asado* chicken, fresh fish tacos, and a grilled steak burrito with refried beans and melted cheese. The place has been discovered, however, so expect a line, particularly at lunch.

SHOPPING

Since Santa Barbara's shops are clustered together, you can easily uncover the town's hottest items and best bargains by concentrating on a few key areas. The prime shopping center lies along State Street, particularly between the 600 and 1300 blocks.

Paseo Nuevo is, literally, a new paseo—a mall, really, with department stores, chain shops, and a few home-grown merchants lining a tastefully designed Spanish style pedestrian promenade. ~ 651 Paseo Nuevo; 805-963-2202, fax 805-564 4239; www.sbmall.com.

La Arcada Court is another spiffy mall done in Spanish style. The shops, along the upper lengths of State Street, are more chic and contemporary than they are elsewhere. Santa Barbara Baggage Company (805-966-2888) sells luggage, handbags, wallets, business bags, and gifts. Closed Sunday. ~ 1114 State Street.

Near the corner of State and Cota streets is the center for vintage clothing. **Yellowstone Clothing** features Hawaiian shirts, used Levi's, and other old time favorites. ~ 527 State Street; 805-963-9609.

The **Territory Ahead** is where the outdoorsy set goes for high-quality men's and women's clothing. The clothes are loose and comfortable, the colors muted, and the styling practical. The company's flagship store has all the latest styles, but the outlet is where the bargains are. ~ Flagship Store: 515 State Street, 805-962-5558 ext. 181; Outlet: 400 State Street, 805-962-5558 ext. 185; www.territoryahead.com.

3D Studio Gallery specializes in, what else, 3-D art. The gallery features the works of Charles Fazzino, an artist best known for his 3-D renderings of various cities and celebrities. Besides limited edition 3-D serigraphs, the gallery sells accessory items such as handpainted ties, jewelry, and puzzles. ~ 529 State Street; 805-730-9109, fax 805-730-9147; www.fazzino.com/3dstudio.htm.

Nothing smells or feels better than fine leather, and at **Crispin Leather** you'll be surrounded by plenty of it.

Sit Up and Beg

A bakery for dogs? Hey, dogs deserve treats too. And all the doggie treats at **Three Dog Bakery** are fresh-baked, all natural, and "paw-sitively yummy." If you have your pooch along, he or she can sniff up the other canine clientele at the bakery's Doggie Bar. ~ 727 State Street; 805-962-8220; www.threedog.com.

Specializing in quality leather products for almost 40 years, this is the place to go for Euro-comfort footwear and other fine leather accessories. This is also the place in town to go for those fabulously comfortable Birkenstock sandals and shoes. ~ 18 West Anapamu Street; 805-966-2510, fax 805-568-1856.

If the romance of Santa Barbara inspires a proposal, nowhere will you find a lovelier engagement ring than at **Bryant & Sons, Ltd.** The jewelry is of the very highest quality and includes names like Tiffany, as well as their original creations. ~ 812 State Street; 805-966-9187, 800-552-4367; www.sbweb.com/bryants/about.htm.

For a New Age shopping experience, **Spirit's Path** is the answer. The store specializes in spiritual and metaphysically oriented gifts and alternative medicines. Items sold to soothe the soul and nurture the spirit include spiritual icons, incense, books, music, and natural medicines, and body care products. ~ 506 State Street; 805-962-2023; www.spiritspath.com.

Wendy Foster/State Street is where the younger well-heeled, style-conscious Santa Barbara woman shops. This airy store features upscale, au courant women's wear with plenty of panache. Expensively hip, styles are creative and eye-catching. Those on a limited budget might consider

Odd-itorium

Scavenge is an edgy little shop that sell reasonably priced items that run the gamut from silly to bizarre. This is undoubtedly the only place in Santa Barbara where you can buy a niobium captive ring, a Rasta red-yellow-and-green-striped light bulb, or a toddler's bride costume. ~ 418 State Street; 805-564-2000; www.scavengeinc.com.

buying one spectacular splurge item here. ~ 833 State Street; 805-966-2276; www.wendyfoster.com.

Morninglory Music is a happening place simply throbbing with sound. This is where to go to buy or sell new and used CDs, DVDs, vinyl, and cassettes, most at discounted prices. Used CDs can be tested at a listening station and any skips buffed out by a store employee on a machine in the back. ~ 1014 State Street; 805-966-0266.

If Santa Barbara and the surrounding area is so beguiling that you'd like to take a little slice of it home with

PICTURE-PERFECT
Specialty shops

you, stop by **Delphine Gallery**. As well as original pieces by local and regional artists working in different medias, the gallery sells limited-edition prints. ~ 1324 State Street; 805-962-6625.

NIGHTLIFE

The State Street strip in downtown Santa Barbara offers several party places. **Zelo** has dancing to a variety of dee-jay music including hip-hop, disco, funk, and salsa. Live bands perform outside on weekends. Cover. ~ 630 State Street; 805-966-5792.

Up at **Acapulco Restaurant**, in La Arcada Court, you can sip a margarita next to an antique wooden bar or out on the patio. ~ 1114 State Street; 805-963-3469.

You can also consider the **Lobero Theatre**, which presents dance, drama, concerts, and lectures. ~ 33 East Cañon Perdido Street; 805-963-0761; www.lobero.com.

Elsie's loyal following give it a neighborhood bar feel. Rooms are color coded with comfortable couches, there's a pool table, and on warm nights customers spill out onto the large patio. ~ 117 West De la Guerra Street; 805-963-4503.

SOhO is a happening place where you can listen to live music that ranges from funk to jazz, seven nights a week. The outside patio fills up fast on summer evenings, and the bartenders are rumored to be the friendliest in town. ~ 1221 State Street, Suite 205; 805-962-7776; www.sohosb.com.

The young and the hip frequent the **Wildcat Lounge**, with its quirkily retro '50s red-vinyl and leopard-print decor. One of Santa Barbara's hottest nightspots, the lounge is frequently packed with trendy locals listening to live music. ~ 15 West Ortega Street; 805-962-7970.

Like a little bit of Dublin in downtown Santa Barbara, **Dargan's Irish Pub & Restaurant** is the place to hang out with pals over a pint of Guinness, shoot a few rounds of pool, or wolf down a big bowl of Irish stew. ~ 18 East Ortega Street; 805-568-0702; www.dargans.com.

For a taste of brewed-on-the-premises local beers, head for the **Santa Barbara Brewing Company**. Specialty beers include everything from Santa Barbara Blonde light ale to State Street stout. The restaurant features hearty fare, but the real reason to visit is the beer. ~ 501 State Street; 805-730-1040; www.sbbrewco.com.

Santa Barbara may be a small city, but it is anything but a cultural wasteland. From classical to blues, from innovative to traditional and from imposing to intimate, the city's community-supported performing arts organizations can deliver.

The oldest of the performing arts organizations is the **Santa Barbara Choral Society**, a 100-member choral group conceived in 1948. ~ 805-965-6577; www.sbchoral.org.

Founded in 1994, **Opera Santa Barbara** mounts a full-scale production each spring and fall. Its home in the historic Lobero Theatre contains just 650 seats, making every performance an intimate affair. ~ 805-898-3890, 800-563-7181; www.operasb.com.

The **Ensemble Theatre Company**, established in 1979, is the city's longest-running professional theater company. Housed in a historic 140-seat theater in the Presidio District, the company offers a diverse repertoire that includes cutting-edge contemporary works and innovative interpretations of the classics. ~ 805-962-8606; www.ensembletheatre.com.

For 25 years the **Santa Barbara Chamber Orchestra** has played to packed houses. Top-notch local musicians play classical chamber music with renowned guest soloists. ~ 805-966-2441; www.sbco.org.

The **Santa Barbara Symphony** was founded in 1953, in conjunction with the University of California Santa Barbara music department. Besides regular performances of more traditional symphonies, the organization has a composer-in-residence program recognizing modern composers whose works are included in the symphony's programs. ~ 805-898-9626; www.thesymphony.org.

Since 1994 **State Street Ballet** has received critical acclaim for its performances both at home and on tour.

Meet the Press

A locals bar, **The Press Room** is a cross between a European pub and an American dive. Tiny, the place broadcasts late-night foreign sports matches, has a great jukebox, and caters to a cast of regulars. ~ 15 East Ortega Street; 805-963-8121.

Director Rodney Gustafson strives to blend classical technique with original and innovative choreography to achieve ballet that combines compelling drama with elegant dance. ~ 805-965-6066; www.statestreetballet.com.

The **Santa Barbara Blues Society** was founded in 1977 by a couple of local blues aficionados who wanted to bring live blues music to Santa Barbara. Over the years the membership has grown to over 400 blues fans and the organization has hosted over 130 performers, including such greats as Mose Allison and Etta James, in more than 160 concerts. ~ 805-897-0060; www.sbblues.org.

3.

The Waterfront

he Public Beach, held sacred to California residents, is a nightmare for resort and restaurant owners. Although much of the Southern California coast is lined with concrete sand boxes that only hint of natural beaches, Santa Barbara has managed to develop one of California's most breathtaking beachfront strips without spoiling it. Today, the city's beachfront is a bustling tourist mecca comprised of low-rise, mission-style resorts, inns, restaurants, and surf shops along the north side of Cabrillo Boulevard. Across the road palm fringed parks open onto a white-sand beach that borders the Pacific.

Although, during the 1920s, these beaches became vital attractions for Santa Barbara's tourist industry, today's glitzy wa-

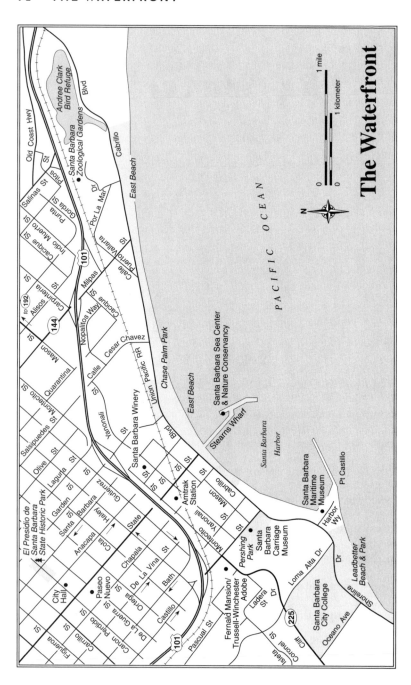

The Waterfront

PACIFIC OCEAN

N

0   1 mile
0   1 kilometer

Old Coast Hwy

Andree Clark
Bird Refuge

Santa Barbara
Zoological Gardens

Cabrillo Blvd

solid St

Salinas St

Gorda St

Punta Gorda St

Cacique St

Indio Muerto St

Carpinteria St

Alisos St

Mason St

Quarantina St

Montecito St

Salsipuedes St

Olive St

Laguna St

Garden St

Santa Barbara St

Cota St

Anacapa St

State St

Chapala St

De La Vina St

Bath St

Castillo St

Ortega St

De La Guerra St

Canon Perdido St

Carrillo St

Figueroa St

to 192

144

225

101

101

El Presidio de
Santa Barbara
State Historic Park

City Hall

Paseo Nuevo

Fernald Mansion/
Trussell-Winchester
Adobe

Pascual St

Ladera Dr

Coronel St

Isleta St

Cliff Dr

Oceano Ave

Santa Barbara
City College

Leadbetter
Beach & Park

Shoreline Dr

Loma Alta Dr

Pershing Park

Santa Barbara
Carriage Museum

Harbor Wy

Santa Barbara
Maritime Museum

Pt Castillo

Santa Barbara
Harbor

Stearns Wharf

Santa Barbara Sea Center
& Nature Conservancy

East Beach

Chase Palm Park

East Beach

Santa Barbara Winery

Union Pacific RR

Cabrillo Blvd

Yanonali St

Calle Cesar Chavez

Nopalitos Way

Cacique St

Milpas St

Calle Puerto Vallarta

Por La Mar Dr

Amtrak Station

Cabrillo St

Mason St

Yanonali St

Montecito St

Gutierrez St

Haley St

Pershing Park

terfront bares little resemblance to the beaches of
the past. In 1872 Stearns Wharf stretched its pilings
into Santa Barbara's coastal waters and connected
the city with the lucrative shipping and passenger
traffic of the Pacific. The wharf drastically changed
the face and future of Santa Barbara and the waterfront that exists today would not be the same
without it. The priceless plots of land that look out
to sea over Cabrillo Boulevard were, during the
19th century, worth about 75 cents an acre. Need-
less to say, with waterfront property in the millions
today, times have changed along Santa Barbara's
waterfront.

Few would sneer at the contemporary scenery that has replaced the cranes and bulky ships that once creaked about the breakwaters in decades past. Santa Barbara's waterfront has become a vivacious center for tourists, celebrities and sun-seeking beach bums. The strip of shops and beaches may not be the ideal place for an intimate stroll but this crowded hotspot is one of Santa Barbara's best locales for food, fun, and a whole lot of sun.

SIGHTS

Santa Barbara's waterfront holds a rich collection of activities centered around the region's maritime history and diverse aquatic and coastal life. This strip of beachfront is also concentrated tightly enough to allow you to see all the sights without ever jumping in the car.

An excellent place to begin your coastal trek is **Chase Palm Park**. Here a constant stream of joggers, bicyclists, and rollerbladers whiz along the path that cuts through the grassy, palm-lined, beachside strip of land along Cabrillo Boulevard, but most have no idea that this is actually part of a city park. Chase Palm Park has areas on both sides of Cabrillo Boulevard, with the more traditional park area on the city side. While the active set are tossing Frisbees and kicking soccer balls around beachside, those who want to chill out should head across the street. At the cityside part of the park you can ride on an antique carousel, stroll along the manicured walks, hang out by the pond, or watch the younger set clammer around on the playground. On balmy summer evenings musical events take place in the outdoor music pavilion. ~ 323 East Cabrillo Boulevard; 805-962-8956.

Chase Palm Park.

Every Sunday morning, the greenbelt at **East Beach** next to Stearns Wharf turns into an outdoor art show. Dozens of local and regional artists exhibit their artwork, photography, jewelry, and crafts. Quality varies, of course,

Text continued on page 78.

The Funk Zone

About as far removed architecturally from Santa Barbara's pristine Spanish style as you can get, what has become known at "The Funk Zone" is a conglomeration of warehouses, Quonset huts, and early 20th-century wood-frame bungalows. The blocks of Helena Avenue and Anacapa Street, stretching from Cabrillo Boulevard to the 101 Freeway, have become perhaps the last bastion in Santa Barbara for struggling artists, misfits, and decidedly non-mainstream businesses. Greedy developers are salivating at the thought of demolishing the area to make way for high-priced condos, but, so far anyway, residents and friends of this little slice of funk in an otherwise picture perfect community have tenaciously fought gentrification.

Start your stroll at one of the area's more high-end businesses, **Italian Pottery Outlet**. Classic glazed and painted pottery, which includes everything from large garden pots to salt and

pepper shakers, is available for as much as 50 percent off the retail price. ~ 19 Helena Avenue; 805-564-7655.

Across the street **Again Books** is a real book lovers bookstore. This is the kind of place where you can spend hours pouring through semi-organized stacks of used books on almost any subject. ~ 16-A Helena Avenue; 805-966-9312.

Next door is Jim O'Mahoney's **Santa Barbara Surfing Museum**. More an experience than a museum, even the front of the place is a trip, with a tiki on a surfboard and a sign declaring the distance from the museum to both the Atlantic (3087 miles) and the Pacific (164 feet) oceans. Inside is one man's wacky assortment of stuff related to surfing and the accompanying lifestyle, including vintage boards, and such Hawaiian memorabilia as ukuleles and hula girls. O'Mahoney shares his collection with the public at no charge on Sunday afternoon unless, of course, the surf's up. ~ 16½ Helena Avenue; 805-962-9048.

Just a breath away on the same side of Helena Avenue is **Jotogo Art Gallery**, with eclectic artwork displayed inside and out. ~ 46 Helena Avenue.

Next door at **Uptown Antiques and Collectables** you can buy anything from an oriental carpet to a vintage Hawaiian shirt out of this warehouse filled with stuff. ~ 52 Helena Avenue; 805-966-1915.

Walk past the auto paint shop, turn right on Mason Street and right again on

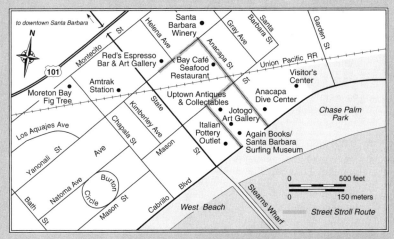

Anacapa Street. Breeze past an eclectic mix of arty and industrial businesses on your way to the **Anacapa Dive Center**. Who'd have thought that housed in an old-time Quonset hut was a full-service scuba center, complete with heated pool and hot showers. If you fancy a diving trip to the nearby Channel Islands, this is the place to go for everything from equipment to certification. ~ 22 Anacapa Street; 805-963-8917.

For a yummy lunch in charming surroundings, turn right out of the dive shop and head to **Bay Café Seafood Restaurant**. Wolfing down a baked oyster sandwich or mahi mahi tacos on the outside patio of this off-the-beaten-track eatery is the ultimate in relaxation and should refuel you for the rest of the stroll. ~ 131 Anacapa Street; 805-963-2215.

Fortified with food, head up the street for a little winetasting at **Santa Barbara Winery**. In this location for 40 years, this isn't simply a tasting room and store, but the place where all the winery's white wines are made and where the barrel aging, bottling, and shipping is done. ~ 202 Anacapa Street; 805-963-3633.

If coffee is more your thing, take Yanonali Street back to Helena Avenue and stop in at **Red's Espresso Bar and Art Gallery**. A throwback to the coffeehouses of yore, the place is the ultimate in funk, with crazy wall decorations and garage sale–type furniture. At night there are poetry readings, live music, and impromptu happenings, and its loyal following will tell you that the coffee beats anything a trendy café could produce. ~ 211 Helena Avenue; 805-966-5906.

Unless you want to negotiate the railroad tracks, head back to the car via State or Anacapa streets.

The Story Behind Stearns

An estimated 5 million people a year walk, shop, and eat on **Stearns Wharf**, yet most haven't a clue as to the origin of its name. Visitors can thank John Peck Stearns for this picturesque Santa Barbara landmark, which was built years before automobiles bounced blunkity-blunk over its heavy wooden boards. When Stearns moved to Santa Barbara in 1867, the town was more or less cut off from the rest of the country due to the natural boundaries of mountains and sea. Stearns, who owned a lumberyard at the foot of State Street, realized that a long wharf would allow ocean ships to tie up at low tide, making the town more accessible and the delivery of goods easier. In 1872 the wharf was completed and, despite a slew of disasters including several devastating fires, a collision with a Chinese junk, a near collapse from heavy foot traffic, a tornado, and several severe storms, the wharf survives today, making it the oldest working wood wharf in California. ~ www.stearnswharf.org.

but the setting is unbeatable. ~ Cabrillo Boulevard at State Street.

For a taste of sea air and salt spray, walk out along **Stearns Wharf**. From the end of this wooden pier you can gaze back at Santa Barbara, realizing how aptly author Richard Henry Dana described the place: "The town is finely situated, with a bay in front, and an amphitheater of hills behind." Favored by local anglers, the wharf is also noted for the **Sea Center**, a working marine laboratory where visitors can engage in the work of scientist who study, monitor, and determine how best to protect the ocean. Admission. ~ At the foot of State Street, 211 Stearns Wharf; 805-682 4711, fax 805-569-3170.

If you tire of walking, remember that Stearns Wharf is the departure point for the **Santa Barbara Old Town Trolley**, an old-fashioned vehicle that carries visitors along the waterfront, through the downtown area, and out to the mission. Fee. ~ 805-965-0353, fax 805-965 1075; www.sbtrolley.com.

Back along the waterfront, Cabrillo Boulevard continues to the **yacht harbor**, where 1200 pleasure boats, some worth millions, are moored. The walkway leads past yawls, ketches, sloops, and fishing boats to the breakwater. From here you can survey the fleet and take in the surrounding mountains and ocean. ~ West Cabrillo Boulevard and Castillo Street.

PICTURE-PERFECT
Spots to watch the sunset

1. **Longboards,** *p. 90*
2. **Cabrillo Inn's upper decks,** *p. 88*
3. **Hendry's (Arroyo Burro) Beach,** *p. 110*
4. **Brophy Brothers Restaurant & Clam Bar,** *p. 89*
5. **Shoreline Park,** *p. 109*

Cabrillo Boulevard.   Across from the marina the old Naval Reserve Center building houses the **Santa Barbara Maritime Museum.** Covering all marine aspects of California's Central Coast, from oil spills to surfing, the museum focuses as much as possible on the Santa Barbara area. There are many in-

teractive exhibits for children, such as a sportsfishing

Santa Barbara Water Taxi

The **Santa Barbara Water Taxi** is a too-cute, little tug-type boat, with a smiling face on its yellow bow, that ferries folks back and forth from the

wharf to the harbor. Captain Fred is at the helm of "Lil Toot" and will gladly let kids try steering the boat and sounding its steam whistle. Trips run every half hour and are a great way for landlubbers to have a short sea-going experience at bargain prices ($2 for adults, $1 for kids). ~ 805-896-6900; e-mail info@sbwatertaxi.com.

Calling All Birders

Besides spotting seabirds by the hundreds at East Beach, bird-watchers can add more species to their sightings by popping across the street to the **Andree Clark Bird Refuge**. Known locally as simply "The Bird Refuge," the area was originally a salt marsh, receiving fresh water from a local creek. In the 1880s, however, the building of the railroad re-routed the creek, thus cutting off the marsh's supply of fresh water. In the late 1920s the area was restored to provide a refuge for wild birds that would either reside there permanently or stop off during migration. While there are always plenty of resident ducks and mallards splashing around the 29-acre lake, birdwatchers will be able to spot a variety of other feathered friends, including heron, grebes, cormorants, egrets, kestrels, and meadowlarks. ~ 1400 East Cabrillo Boulevard.

simulator, as well as some treats for adults that include the state-of-the-art audiovisual Munger Theater, shaped like a ship's hull, which shows films throughout the day, and an internet-based weather kiosk to let you know if it's a good day for sailing or a storm's a brewin'. If a volunteer is on duty on the observation deck, take the lobby elevator to the fourth floor for stunning views of the harbor and Channel Islands. ~ 113 Harbor Way, Suite 190; 805-962-8404, fax 805-962-7634; www.sbmm.org, e-mail museum@sbmm.org.

Backtracking to the eastern stretch of Cabrillo Boulevard you'll encounter the **Andree Clark Bird Refuge**, a placid lagoon that hints of Santa Barbara's wetland past.

Painter at Andree Clark Bird Refuge.

During the southern migration the refuge is filled with geese and other freshwater fowl. There are three tree-tufted islands in the center and a trail around the park. ~ 1400 East Cabrillo Boulevard.

For an up close and personal look at some of the antique carriages that roll down State Street during the Fiesta Parade, stop in at the **Santa Barbara Carriage Museum**. Some of the more unusual carriages are the patty wagon used in a Clint Eastwood movie, a hearse, and a circus wagon. In addition to carriages, the museum showcases over 50 saddles once belonging to California's cowboys of the silver screen like Ronald Reagan, Will Rogers, and Clark Gable. The restoration and preservation of the vehicles takes place on the premises using the technology of the Old West, a forge and anvil to make tools and car-

riage parts. ~ 129 Castillo Street; 805-962-8101; www.
carriagemuseum.org, e-mail info@carriagemuseum.org.

Examples of two diverse 19th-century architectural
styles, the **Fernald Mansion** and the **Trussell-Winchester
Adobe** sit side by side on a large piece of property. The
formal Queen Anne–style Fernald Mansion was built by
Judge Charles Fernald; elegantly furnished with
Victorian antiques and surrounded by a lovely flowering
garden. Facing the street, the more modest Trussell
Winchester Adobe, was built about ten years earlier by
Captain Horatio Gates Trussell in a eclectic mixture of
architectural styles. Adobe was combined with, appropriately enough for a sea captain's residence, timber and
brass salvaged from a wrecked ship. ~ 414 West Montecito Street; 805-966-1601, fax 805-966-1603.

On the same route you can find the **Moreton Bay Fig
Tree**, a century-old giant with branches that spread 160
feet. This magnificent specimen stands as the
largest tree of its kind in the U.S. ~
Chapala and Montecito streets.

Finally, if you just aren't satis
fied with the exotic history, flora,
and fauna of the region head
over to **Santa Barbara Zoological Gardens,** with its minia-
ture train ride and population
of monkeys, lions, elephants,
giraffes, and even more exotic
birds. Admission. ~ 500 Ninos
Drive; 805-962-6310; www.sbzoo.
org, e-mail zooinfo@sbzoo.org.

LODGING

Old Yacht Club Inn

431 Corona del Mar Drive
805-962-1277, 800-676-1676, fax 805-962-3989
www.oldyachtclubinn.com, e-mail info@oldyachtclubinn.com
5 rooms
DELUXE TO ULTRA-DELUXE

The Old Yacht Club Inn is two inns in one. The main facility is a 1912 California craftsman–style house with five rooms. There is a cozy parlor downstairs where wine and cheese are served in the evening. Next door, in a 1927 vintage stucco, there are seven guest rooms with private baths. Some have been decorated by different families and feature personal photographs and other heirlooms, other rooms feature elegant European decor. The inn is just one block from East Beach, serves a full gourmet breakfast and provides bikes, beach chairs, and towels to guests. Occasionally, owner Nancy Donaldson

Natural Landscaping

From the rim of the sea to the peaks of surrounding mountains, the Santa Barbara coastline is coated with a complex variety of plant life. Several plant communities flourish along the shore, each clinging to a particular niche in the environment. Blessed with a cool, moderate climate, coastal vegetation is continually misted by sea spray and must contend with more salt in its veins. On the beaches and along the dunes are the herbs, vines, and low shrubs of the coastal strand community. Among their numbers are beach primrose, sand verbena, beach morning-glory, and sea figs, those tenacious succulents that run along the ground sprouting magenta flowers and literally carpeting the coast. Characterized by leathery leaves that retain large quantities of water, sea figs are the plant world's answer to the camel.

offers an elegantly prepared five-course gourmet Saturday dinner to guests. The inn books far in advance on these nights, but it's well worth the wait.

The Villa Rosa Inn
15 Chapala Street
805-966-0851, fax 805-962-7159
www.villarosainnsb.com, e-mail info@villarosainnsb.com
18 rooms
DELUXE TO ULTRA-DELUXE

For chic surroundings there is The Villa Rosa Inn. Built during the 1930s in Spanish palazzo fashion, it was originally an apartment house. Today it is an 18-room inn with rawwood furnishings and private baths. There's a pool and spa in the courtyard. Guests mingle over continental breakfast and afternoon wine and cheese, then settle into plump armchairs around a tile fireplace with port and sherry in the evening. The spacious rooms, some with fireplaces, are pleasantly understated and located half a block from the beach.

The Villa Rosa Inn.

Hotel Oceana Santa Barbara
202 West Cabrillo Boulevard
805-965-4577, 800-965-9776, fax 805-965-9937
www.hoteloceanasantabarbara.com
122 rooms
DELUXE TO ULTRA-DELUXE

Hotel Oceana is definitely the place to go if you want to feel like you're on the French Riviera without having to actually fly 11 hours to get there. A boutique hotel

with all of the upscale amenities, gardens are lush with colorful blooms, balconies are draped in honeysuckle, and the rooms are decorated in designer fabrics in clear sunny colors with patterns reminiscent of Provence. There are sun terraces, two pools, a fitness center, and a spa. It's a lovely property, but, considering the room price, it seems a bit chintzy to charge $10 for the continental breakfast.

Casa del Mar
18 Bath Street
850-963-4418, 800-433-3097, fax 805-966-4240
www.casadelmar.com, e-mail reservations@casadelmar.com
21 rooms
DELUXE TO ULTRA-DELUXE

Casa del Mar is the perfect answer for those who are looking for bed-and-breakfast style with hotel privacy. The architecture is Santa Barbara Spanish, and each of the inn's accommodations has a private entrance that opens up into flowering gardens and tiled pathways. Room types run the gamut from an individually decorated bedroom to a two-room suite with full kitchen and fireplace. In the extras department, besides a whirlpool spa and sundeck, there's an all-you-can-eat buffet-style continental breakfast in the morning, and wine and cheese in the evening.

Inn by the Harbor
433 West Montecito Street
805-963-7851, 800-962-1986, fax 805-962-9428
www.sbhotels.com
43 rooms
MODERATE TO DELUXE

Despite the Inn by the Harbor not really being by the harbor, it is a pleasant property within easy walking distance of the waterfront. The inn and its grounds exude the Santa Barbara style with lots of white stucco, graceful arches, red tile, and a flower-festooned courtyard. Pine furniture and quilt-like bedspreads give the rooms a country feel. Amenities include a deluxe continental

Inn-dulgence

In a residential area a few blocks from the beach, right next door to the historic Fernald Mansion and Trussell-Winchester Adobe, **The Orchid Inn** bed and breakfast occupies a two-story Colonial revival craftsman bungalow built in 1920 and its adjoining three-story carriage house. The nine rooms, painted and furnished in neutral tones with deeply colored accents, are elegant. The owners are eager to please and offer a full breakfast featuring quiches, frittatas, or cornbread French toast, as well as complimentary afternoon wine and cheese. ~ 420 West Montecito Street; 805-965-2333, 877-722-3657, fax 805-962-4907; www.orchidinnatsb.com, e-mail info@orchidinnatsb.com. DELUXE TO ULTRA-DELUXE.

Cabrillo Inn at the Beach.

breakfast, wine and cheese at cocktail hour, and cookies and milk for a before-bed snack.

Cabrillo Inn at the Beach

931 East Cabrillo Boulevard
805-966-1641, 800-648-6708, fax 805-965-1623
www.cabrillo-inn.com, e-mail info@cabrillo-inn.com
40 rooms
MODERATE TO DELUXE

This two- and three-story 1950s-style motel is located across from East Beach. The place isn't fancy, but the grounds are immaculate with brightly colored flowers and a manicured lawn, the rooms are pleasantly furnished, there are two large swimming pools, and the view from the upper deck is awesome. Rooms at the back can be dark so if light is an issue, ask for a room toward the front overlooking one of the pools. A generous complimentary continental breakfast and a morning paper comes with the room, and the staff is willing and helpful. The truth is, considering the cost of some of the surrounding hotels and motels, Cabrillo Inn is a bargain.

DINING

Brophy Brothers Restaurant & Clam Bar
119 Harbor Way
805-966-4418
e-mail brophybrothers@prodigy.net
BUDGET TO DELUXE

For a scent of Santa Barbara salt air with your lunch or dinner, Brophy Brothers Restaurant & Clam Bar is the spot. Located out on the breakwater, overlooking the marina, mountains, and open sea, it features a small dining room and patio. If you love seafood, it's heaven; if not, then fate has cast you in the wrong direction. The clam bar serves all manner of clam and oyster concoctions, and the restaurant is so committed to fresh fish they print a new menu daily to tell you what the boats brought in. When I was there the daily fare included fresh snapper, shark, scampi, salmon, sea bass, halibut, and mahi mahi.

The Harbor Restaurant
210 Stearns Wharf
805-963-3311, fax 805-962-9021
closed Sunday
MODERATE TO DELUXE, MODERATE at
   Longboards (upstairs)

For dazzling waterfront views it's tough to beat The Harbor Restaurant on Stearns Wharf. During its decades of business the restaurant has gone through some major remodelings but has always retained its nautical theme. A word of caution—if you're looking for award-winning cuisine forget The Harbor. The food is not the main attraction here, the view is. For a less formal atmosphere, with even better views, head upstairs to Longboards. This happening surf-themed bar serves up frosty margaritas, unlimited shell-them-yourself peanuts, and regulation American-style pub grub.

Fish House
101 East Cabrillo Boulevard
805-966-2112
MODERATE TO DELUXE

The Fish House, Santa Barbara Shellfish Company's more upscale sister restaurant, is a cozy place with dark polished wooden floors, an open kitchen, tabletops covered in laminated nautical charts, aquariums, and other fish-related touches. The seafood here is every bit as fresh and delicious as its more casual wharf restaurant, but dishes are a bit more creative. There are almost always two types of fresh oysters—just as fresh as they come—and local fish is used whenever possible. Yummy creations include crusted sea bass on crispy polenta with a generous helping of fresh and perfectly cooked asparagus, whole live lobsters, and succulent and sinfully rich oysters Rockefeller. Even if the night is coolish, heat lamps keep the patio—which faces the ocean—warm, making it a lovely spot to watch the twinkling stars over the water.

Waterfront Grill & Endless Summer Café

113 Harbor Way
805-564-1200 (grill), 805-564-4666 (bar/café), fax 805-564-3445
www.waterfrontgrill.net
MODERATE TO DELUXE

Located in the former Naval Reserve Center building at the marina, the second story Endless Summer Café and its more formal ground floor offshoot, the Waterfront Grill, is Santa Barbara's hottest new seafood duo. Surfing fans will eat up the memorabilia from the movie *Endless Summer* that decorate the café, where the terrace overflows with people when the weather's warm. Both restaurants buy their fish right off the fishing boats that are moored just steps away. Fish specials feature the best of the day's catch and may include such tantalizing choices as Santa Barbara spiny lobster with rock shrimp ravioli, and local halibut crusted in bread crumbs, sesame, and black pepper.

PICTURE-PERFECT
Places to Sample Seafood

1. **Santa Barbara Shellfish Company,** *p. 92*
2. **Waterfront Grill & Endless Summer Café,** *p. 91*
3. **Brophy Brothers Restaurant & Clam Bar,** *p. 89*
4. **Enterprise Fish Co.,** *p. 93*
5. **Bay Café Seafood Restaurant and Fish Market,** *p. 94*

Santa Barbara Shellfish Company

230 Stearns Wharf
805-966-6676, fax 805-963-1802
BUDGET

It may look unpretentious, but this little seafood restaurant on Stearns Wharf has star power, having appeared on both the "Today Show" and the Food Network. Serving up some of the freshest seafood in town since 1979, Santa Barbara Shellfish Company is pure casual with a seafood bar inside and outdoor dining at picnic tables overlooking the water. South-of-the-border-style ceviche comes with homemade tortilla chips, you can choose live crab and lobster out of the tank, there are all sorts of shellfish specials, and the clam chowder is to die for. If you

Chumash Canoes

Whether catching dinner or trading with nearby villages, a Santa Barbara Chumash Indian depended on his *tomol*, or plank canoe. These sturdy seaworthy vessels were constructed of driftwood or redwood and averaged in length from 8 to 30 feet. Planks used for both bottom and sides were glued in place with *yop*, a mixture of pine pitch and tar, then each plank was attached to the one below using plant-fiber string tied through drilled holes. Finally, holes and seams were sealed with more *yop* and the boat was sanded, painted and decorated. While the 1850s marked the last time a *tomol* was made for fishing, in 1913 an anthropologist specializing in the Chumash culture, John Harrington, took copious notes as Fernando Librado, an elderly Chumash man, demonstrated how a *tomol* was crafted. The resulting canoe is on display at the Santa Barbara Museum of Natural History. Harrington's notes have been used by the handful of 20th-century boat builders who have constructed their own *tomols*, including the 26½-foot *Helek*. Built by local boat builders and members of the Quabajai Chumash Indian Association of Santa Barbara out of driftwood, the *Helek* was successfully launched and, crewed by Chumash descendants, proved itself seaworthy.

eat ocean-side though, beware of nervy local seagulls who may decide to sample your lunch when you're not looking.

Enterprise Fish Co.
225 State Street
805-962-3313, fax 805-962-7802
www.enterprisefishco.com
MODERATE TO DELUXE

Decorated in early warehouse, Enterprise Fish Co. is where friends and families scarf generous portions of seafood in a casual atmosphere. To lend a nautical air to the industrial interior, the-one-that-got-away-sized fish trophies dangle from the exposed duct piping, and black-and-white fishing photos adorn the walls. The oyster bar is hopping during weekday happy hour (4 to 7 p.m.) when well drinks and house wines go for $3, draught beer for $2.50, and the appetizer specials include such bargains as oysters for $.75 a pop, California crab cakes for $3.95, and steamed clams for $6.95. Preparation is simple here, specializing mostly in the freshest fish available grilled over mesquite-wood charcoal in an open kitchen, which dominates the middle of the restaurant. Lobster lovers won't want to miss the Monday and Tuesday special. If you prefer crab, come on Wednesday and Thursday.

East Beach Grill
1188 East Cabrillo Boulevard
805-965-8805, fax 805-965-2585
BUDGET

There's nowhere to better experience the laid-back California beach scene than the East Beach Grill. Shaded by umbrellas, swim-suited barefooted diners languish at tables just steps from the sand as they watch the passing parade of tanned, buffed, and muscled roller bladers, bicyclists, and joggers. The ordering counter and grill are housed in part of an early 20th-century bathhouse, pho-

Seafood Fusion

For years this was the location of Castagnola's Fish Market, the favorite place in Santa Barbara to buy fresh seafood. Today it is **Bay Café Seafood Restaurant and Fish Market**, a romantic little off-the-beaten-path restau-

rant where you won't get an ocean view, but you will get some great pasta and seafood dishes served in intimate surroundings. The simple wooden furniture, colorful one-of-a-kind artwork, and bright blue accents reflect the owner's South American experience as a restaurateur in Ecuador. At night the patio is alight with candles and strings of tiny white lights. All the pasta is made fresh and includes entrées such as charbroiled lobster tail over pasta in alfredo sauce, and shrimp served over ricotta cheese ravioli pasta in rice vinegar sauce. And, though considerably smaller than the original, there is still a fish market specializing in the freshest seafood to go. ~ 131 Anacapa Street; 805-963-2215, fax 805-963-2136; www.restauranteur.com/baycafe. MODERATE TO DELUXE.

tos on the wall are of pleasant pastel-toned beach scenes, and, besides the sand-side setting, there's a small room for indoor dining. Breakfasts are particularly popular here, especially on the weekends, with two of the tastiest choices being multigrain pancakes and stick-to-your-ribs oatmeal. Open weekdays 6 a.m. to 6 p.m. and weekends 6 a.m. to 7 p.m.

East Beach Grill.

Shoreline Beach Café

801 Shoreline Drive
805-568-0064, fax 805-564-8754
BUDGET

The Shoreline Beach Café is about as close to the sand as you can get and still have someone else do the cooking. It's also the only beach café with a glass-enclosed heated deck for those days when the temperatures are cool, but the view still spectacular. The food is basic, including burgers, fish sandwiches, and salads, but it's the perfect place for a casual meal with an oceanfront view. Also a great spot to watch the sunset at cocktail hour, Shoreline serves sunset specials from 4 to 6 p.m., Monday through Thursday. Friday night's tropical drink specials and free pupus pack the place on a summer evening.

SHOPPING

The **Surf-N-Wear's Beach House** is a warehouse-sized store with a positively overwhelming selection of beachwear, not to mention surfing-related objects and memorabilia, and the boards themselves. It's also the home of Santa Barbara Surf Shop, which started in Summerland in 1962, when it would close its doors when the surf was up. Though the Surf-N-Wear doesn't close down on perfect surfing days today, it's guaranteed to outfit you to hit the beach, whether it be on a board or as a spectator. ~ 10 State Street; 805-963-1281; www.surfnwear.com.

Serious surfing aficionados will recognize the name Al Merrick as the driving force behind **Channel Island Surfboards**. Since 1969 Merrick and his family have been building innovative quality boards that are used by some of the world's top surfers. Up to 75 boards a day are produced in the manufacturing shop across the street from the company's retail shop, where, besides the boards themselves, there is a full range of beach-type clothing for sale. ~ 29 State Street; 805-966-7213; www.cisurfboards.com.

Help for Hodads (aka Surfing Newbies)

It may appear simple from the safety and solidity of the sand but surfing is a sport rarely conquered by the first-timer paddling out on their own. Just figuring out how to keep the nose from submerging itself can be nasty and dangerous; so if you are thinking about attempting to hang ten and would prefer to keep your body intact and the seawater out of your nose, try a surf lesson. **Santa Barbara Adventure Company**'s expert instructors give novices the benefit of their years of experience riding the waves by offering day-long surfing lessons. Boards and wetsuits are provided, locations vary depending on the day's surf, and instruction is conducted both on the beach and in the water. Day trips for two or more run from 10 a.m. to 3 p.m. and cost $95 per person. ~ 805-452-1942, 888-773-3239, fax 805-560-7218; www.sbadventureco.com, e-mail contact@sbadventureco.com.

With its distinctive logo of, what else, a big black and white St. Bernard–type dog, the Santa Barbara–based **Big Dog Sportswear** sells fun, youthful, casual sports- and active wear for men, women, and children. And this hometown outlet store offers all of the Big Dog quality at discount rates. Appropriately, there's no need to leave Rover in the car while you shop because Big Dog encourages canine participation. ~ 6 East Yanonali Street; 805-963-8728; www.bigdogs.com.

NIGHTLIFE

If for no other reason than the view, The **Harbor Restaurant** is a prime place for the evening. A plate-glass establishment, it sits out on a pier with the city skyline on one side and open ocean on the other. The bar upstairs, Longboards, features sports television and surf videos. ~ 210 Stearns Wharf; 805-963 3311.

BEACHES

Cabrillo Boulevard hugs the shore as it tracks past **East Beach**, Santa Barbara's longest, prettiest strand. With its rows of palm trees, grassy acres, and sunbathing crowds, it's an enchanting spot. East Beach boasts all the amenities beachgoers could wish for, including a beachhouse with showers and lockers. You'll also find a snack bar, a playground, volleyball courts and a picnic area with grill tables. Snaking along the length of the beach is a popular biking/jogging path.

4.

Santa Barbara
Neighborhoods

Santa Barbara may not have the feel of a big city on the whole, but the cultural diversity found within its quaint and quiet neighborhoods is a reflection of the American melting pot found throughout the country.

Until the mid 19th century the city's population was mainly Spanish, Mexican, and Chumash, with the majority of the people living in the downtown area. As more people arrived and the ethnic diversity increased, neighborhoods began to radiate out from the city's center.

The first Anglos arrived in the 1860s and settled on the Westside, which, over the next few decades, developed from grassy farmland into a neighborhood of homes that mirrored architectural styles of the East Coast and Midwest.

While Anglos were settling on the Westside, the lower Eastside was transforming from a barren salt marsh into the city's most ethnically diverse neighborhood. As California grew, Santa Barbara saw an influx of immigrants from every corner of the world and before long enclaves of Mexican, Italian, Chinese, and African-American families sprung up throughout the city's working-class neighborhoods. Today some descendants of these coastal

Mission Santa Barbara.

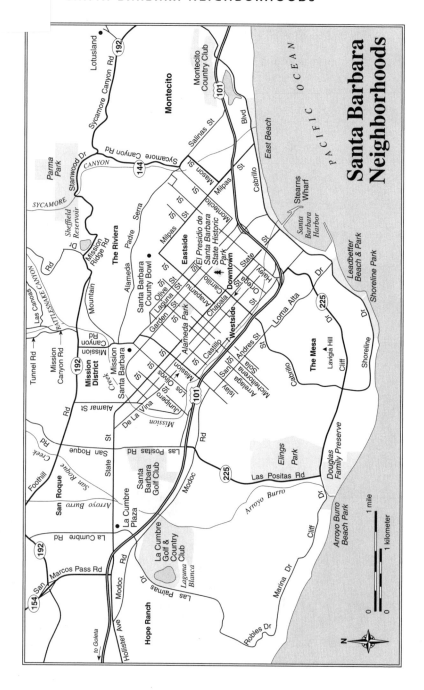

Santa Barbara Neighborhoods

pioneers still live in the same neighborhoods settled by their ancestors more than a century ago.

By the late 19th century, with the less affluent dominating the lower Eastside, the upper Eastside became a bastion of the wealthy. Meanwhile Montecito was turning, thanks to a natural hot springs, from a primarily Spanish settlement into a health haven for the rich.

By the 1920s growth in Santa Barbara was in full swing. Hope Ranch was incorporated into the growing city, homes began to pop up around the Samarkand Hotel, and the San Roque area began to rapidly expand. Two decades later World War II vets started building homes on the Mesa with the help of G.I. loans, making it Santa Barbara's youngest and most middle-class neighborhood.

Hope Ranch.

San Roque   Once nothing more than an open expanse of grassland, the San Roque area, tucked between the foothills and State Street, is as close to suburbia as you're likely to get in Santa Barbara. This is the neighborhood where young mothers can be found wheeling their infants through strip malls full of practical businesses like real estate offices, dry cleaners, and beauty shops. Best of all, ethnic dining options are on the more affordable spectrum.

LODGING

The Sandman Inn
3714 State Street
805-687-2468, 800-350-8174, fax 805-687-6581
www.thesandmaninn.com, e-mail info@thesandmaninn.com
112 rooms
MODERATE

Spread over four acres, The Sandman Inn is a sprawling California ranch–style motel located at the far end

Get Primed
Low-carb dieters will swoon at the giant portions of prime rib served at **Tee-Off**. This old-time Santa Barbara institution has been around since 1956

and looks just about like it did back then. The decor is early cocktail lounge with a golf theme, and the prime rib comes in four sizes—large, huge, gigantic, and "oh my God, it's coming toward us." Besides the prime rib, this is the place to go to see what Santa Barbara dining was like before the invasion of trendy restaurants and chic bistros. Dinner only. ~ 3627 State Street; 805-687-1616, fax 805-687-0526. DELUXE.

Palm Reading

What is the tree that has no branches and sheds little shade? It's the foremost symbol of California—the palm tree. In Santa Barbara, you'll see a staggering variety of palms, including Pindo palms from Paraguay, European hair palms, plume palms from Brazil, blue palms, Washington palms, and the Mexican Erythea. Most common is—surprise—the California palm, the largest native palm in the continental United States. The ubiquitous date palm, nicknamed "pineapple palm" for its trunk's resemblance to the tropical fruit, also lines many streets here.

of State Street in San Roque. Because of the well-landscaped grounds, full of mature plants and trees, this motel seems more intimate than its actual size. The quarters themselves are updated 1950s, with flowered bedspreads and simple light-colored wooden furniture. A continental breakfast is included in the price, and there are two pools and a spa.

DINING

Kyoto
3232 State Street
805-687-1252
no lunch on Sunday
BUDGET TO MODERATE

Perhaps the most traditional of Santa Barbara's Japanese restaurants, Kyoto invites you to dine Western style or "go native." Eating fresh sushi and sipping sake in a private room (with traditional tatami walls, low tables, and cushions) makes eating at Kyoto a cultural *and* culinary experience. Besides sushi there are Japanese specialties such as *nabeyaki udon* noodles with tempura, egg, and

PICTURE-PERFECT
Ethnic Dining

1. **La Super Rica,** *p. 128*
2. **Your Place,** *p. 129*
3. **A Flavor of India,** *p. 104*
4. **Dutch Garden,** *p. 104*
5. **Kyoto,** *p. 103*

chicken, and a tempura combination with shrimp, vegetables, scallops, white fish, and eel.

Dutch Garden
4203 State Street
805-967-4911
closed Sunday and Monday
BUDGET TO MODERATE

Dutch Garden as been on the Santa Barbara restaurant scene since the 1920s, making it one of the city's oldest eateries. Complete with beer garden and a homey dining room, this is the place to experience a little bit of Germany in Southern California. Traditional food is served to strains of oom-pa-pa music and washed down with giant steins of German oktoberfest drafts. Their selection of wurst (as in bratwurst) is impressive and delicious, and the weinerschnitzel is also a winner.

A Flavor of India
3026 State Street
805-682-6561
closed Sunday
BUDGET TO MODERATE

This is where locals come for authentic Indian cuisine. Catering to both vegetarians and carnivores, A Flavor of India serves traditional cooked-from-scratch food at reasonable prices. Tandoori dishes and baked Indian bread are cooked in a traditional coals-on-the-bottom oven. Specialties include chicken *tikka masala* (chicken marinaded in yogurt, garlic, and other spices with a tomato and chile sauce) and curries. The all-you-can-eat lunch buffet is a definite bargain and will set you back less than $10, including beverage and tip.

SHOPPING

Located on upper State Street, **La Cumbre Plaza** is a large open-air shopping complex that features more than 60 restaurants and retail stores. Don't miss the farmers' market held every Wednesday from 11 a.m. to 1 p.m. ~ 120 South Hope Street; 805-687-6458.

The **Seven Day Nursery**, a green oasis at the busy intersection of Las Positas and upper State Street, is home to one of Santa Barbara's finest nurseries. Wander along the narrow stone paths between ornate terra cotta planters, handcrafted iron sculptures and some of Santa Barbara's strangest looking, and smelling, natives. ~ Loreto Plaza, 3301 State Street; 805-687-8036.

Forget the lattes and chamber music ensembles, **Chaucer's Books** is a no-nonsense bookstore that concentrates on its product. One of California's largest full-service independent bookstores, it boasts over 150,000 titles in 400 different sections, in-

Golf on a Budget

Santa Barbara Golf Club transcends the usual municipal course. Besides lovely mountain and ocean views, this par-70, 6014-yard, 18-hole course built in 1958 is, at over 100,000 rounds a year, one of the nation's most played. Conveniently located just minutes from downtown, the rates for 18 holes are affordable ($30 weekdays, $40 weekends—discounts for county residents), and there are plenty of amenities, such as putting green, driving range, golf shop, full-service restaurant, electric carts, and golf clubs rentals. ~ 3500 McCaw Avenue; 805-687-7087.

cluding an impressive children's section. The knowledgeable staff is ready to help you find what you are looking for in this store that is positively bursting its seams with books. ~ Loreto Plaza, 3321 State Street; 805-682-6787, fax 805-682-1129; www.chaucers.booksense.com.

PARKS

Oddly enough, had it not been for the depression, rustic **Stevens Park** would have been the San Roque Country Club golf course. As it is, it is a 25-acre naturally landscaped park, known mainly as being the trailhead for the Stevens Park to Jesusita hike, a gentle two mile roundtrip walk. ~ 258 Canon Drive.

The Mesa   Meaning "table" in Spanish, the Mesa refers to the flat bench of land that hangs over the ocean

along Santa Barbara's southwestern border. Excavations of 6000-year-old Indian villages makes this the city's oldest historical site. A growing shopping district lines Cliff Drive as it slides down toward Shoreline Park and the waterfront while narrow roads meander up and down the Mesa, studded with ranch-style homes, Spanish adobes, and quaint cottages.

DINING

Brown Pelican
2981 Cliff Drive
805-687-4550, fax 805-569-0188
e-mail thepelican@aol.com
breakfast, lunch, and dinner
MODERATE TO ULTRA-DELUXE

On the beach at Arroyo Burro Beach Park is the Brown Pelican. It's a decent restaurant with great ocean views. What more need be said? Sandwiches, salads, hamburgers, and several fresh seafood and pasta dinners are served. Breakfast is available daily until 11 a.m. or later. Trimly appointed and fitted with a wall of plate glass, it looks out upon a sandy beach and tawny bluffs.

Steps to Mesa Beach.

Mesa Café
1972 Cliff Drive
805-966-5303
breakfast, lunch, and dinner
BUDGET TO MODERATE

Located in a low-rise Mesa strip mall, the Mesa Café serves hearty American cuisine in a down-home at-

Mesa Café.

mosphere. Walls are covered in photographs taken by regulars, and the adjacent large bar is a hangout for an eccentric mix of locals. Breakfasts are legendary, with huge omelettes, baked-on-the-premises muffins, and non-stop coffee refills. For lunch, try the carved-off-the-bone hot turkey sandwich with just-mashed potatoes and extra gravy. The late Julia Child frequently breakfasted here on Saturdays—about as good an endorsement as a restaurant can get.

PARKS

The city's biggest and busiest park, **Elings Park** is known locally as Las Positas. The 230 acres, half of which has been left wild, are spread out over one of Santa Barbara's tallest hills, and the panoramic views can be dazzling. For those who like a little action in natural surroundings, there are baseball diamonds, tennis courts, an outdoor amphitheater, and a favorite launching place for hang- and para-gliders. ~ Las Positas Road and Jerry Harwin Parkway; 805-569-5611, fax 805-569-3316; www.elingspark.org.

The **Douglas Family Preserve** is a testimony to a community's determination to keep public land public. Known for years as the Wilcox property, this 70-acre stretch of land overlooking the Pacific Ocean might have

become a housing development if it were not for concerned citizens who did everything from bake sales to formal dinners to raise enough money to buy the property. When the going got rough, actor Michael Douglas kicked in a large dona-tion, named the public open space after his father, Kirk, and the prop-erty belonged to the people of Santa Barbara. ~ Linda Road; 805-564-5418, fax 805-897-2524.

On weekends, **Shoreline Park** is buzzing with skaters, walkers, Frisbee experts, and families. This long narrow grassy park overlook-ing the ocean not only offers some unparalleled views of the harbor, the Channel Islands, and the mountains, but is probably the best place in Santa Barbara to catch a glimpse of a playful dolphin or, when migrating, even a whale or two. A hidden gem of a beach and a tidepool area—when the tide is out—is at the bottom of a narrow flight of wooden stairs. ~ Shoreline Drive and La Marina; 805-564-5418, fax 805-564-5480.

Arroyo Burro Beach Park.

It may be renamed **Arroyo Burro Beach Park**, but to residents it's still Hendry's Beach. And because the park is located away from the developed waterfront area, it's used mostly by locals, particularly surfers, joggers, and dog walkers. The beach is a generous 600 feet long, but there are literally miles of beach to discover beyond this. In fact, at low tide, it's possible to hike to Goleta Beach, a five-mile, one-way trip. ~ 2981 Cliff Drive; 805-687-3714.

The Riviera Navigating Alameda Padre Serra (the tight road between Mission and Sycamore canyons) you'll come across a breathtaking neighborhood originally known as Mission Ridge but aptly renamed The Riviera. Strikingly similar to its European namesake, this two-mile strip boasts some of Santa Barbara's most stunning panoramas. The Spanish villas, cottages, and modern homes aren't huge but the view brings hefty price tags to this elite locale. The Riviera is primarily residential, with the exception of The Brooks Institute, so don't expect to find cafés or shops—the attraction here is purely for the eyes.

SIGHTS

Brooks Institute of Photography is a world-renowned photography school that has trained some of the nation's top photographers, including *National Geographic* un-

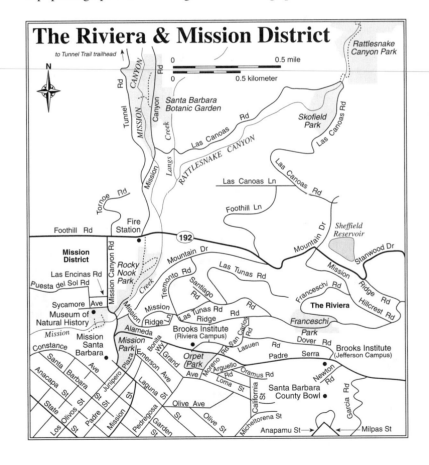

The Riviera & Mission District

Rattlesnake Canyon Park

to Tunnel Trail trailhead

N

0   0.5 mile

0   0.5 kilometer

Santa Barbara Botanic Garden

Skofield Park

MISSION CANYON

Tunnel Rd

Canyon Rd

Mission Creek

Langs Creek

Las Canoas Rd

RATTLESNAKE CANYON

Las Canoas Rd

Las Canoas Ln

Las Canoas Rd

Foothill Ln

Torooe Rd

Fire Station

Foothill Rd

192

Sheffield Reservoir

Mountain Dr

Stanwood Dr

Mission District

Rocky Nook Park

Mountain Dr

Las Tunas Rd

Mission Ridge Rd

Las Encinas Rd

Puesta del Sol Rd

Mission Canyon Rd

Tremonto Rd

Santiago Rd

Franceschi Rd

Hillcrest Rd

Sycamore Ave

Museum of Natural History

Mission Creek

Mission Ridge Ln

Las Tunas Rd

Ridge Rd

The Riviera

Franceschi Park

Mission Constance

Mission

Mission Santa Barbara

Alameda

Mission Park

Bonita

Mission Plaza

Brooks Institute (Riviera Campus)

San Carlos Rd

Dover Rd

Brooks Institute (Jefferson Campus)

Santa Barbara Ave

Juniper

Emerson Ave

Grand Ave

Orpet (Park)

Moreno Rd

Arguello Rd

Lasuen Rd

Padre Serra

Newton Rd

Garcia Rd

Anacapa St

Barbara

Laguna St

Ave

Loma St

Oramus Rd

California St

Santa Barbara County Bowl

State St

Los Olivos St

Padre St

Mission

Pedregosa St

Olive Ave

Garden St

Olive St

Michaeltorena St

Anapamu St→

←Milpas St

derwater photographer David Doubilet and nature photographer George Lepp. There are two campuses in Santa Barbara, the original being in Montecito, the more recent addition on The Riviera. To see some examples of the students' best works, roam the hallways (sometimes referred to as the galleries) of the Riviera campus, where a rotating selection of stunning photographs are displayed. Closed Saturday and Sunday. ~ Jefferson Campus, 1321 Alameda Padre Serra; 805-966-3888, fax 805-585-8001; www.brooks.edu.

Mission District
On the feast of St. Barbara in 1786, Padre Fermin Lausen dedicated the tenth California mission built on the site of a former Chumash village. As the surrounding area developed it became known as the Mission District. Today lovely early-20th-century, Spanish-style homes surround the mission rose garden while neighboring Mission Canyon, home to some of Santa Barbara's most renowned artists, spreads among sprawling California oaks and sycamores. The area vaunts

Indigenous Sports

The Chumash Indians lived in villages dotted around the Santa Barbara area and depended on the sea for their subsistence. Like area residents today, the Chumash enjoyed a variety of vigorous activities. One of the most popular was a team sport called *tikauwich*, or shinny. Somewhat similar to hockey, it was played with curved shinny sticks, which were used to slam a small wooden ball through the opponent's goal post. And not unlike modern-day hockey, participating in a game could be a dangerous proposition. When village played against village, it wasn't unusual for most of the population to be on the field at the same time. As many as 300 people might be swinging wooden sticks on a 300-yard field, and bloody fights broke out regularly between opposing sides. Adding to the excitement was the frenzied betting on the outcome of the match, with half of the profits from the winning side going to the chief of the village hosting the game to pay for the festivities.

the most spectacular historic gardens and parks in the city with an emphasis on California and local species of flora.

SIGHTS

Mission Santa Barbara sits on a knoll overlooking the city. Founded in 1786 and restored in 1820, this twin-towered beauty, known as the "Queen of the Missions," follows a design from an ancient Roman architecture book. The interior courtyard is a colonnaded affair with a central fountain and a graceful flower garden. The chapel itself is quite impressive with a row of wrought iron chandeliers leading to a multicolored altar. There are also museum displays representing the original American Indian population and early-19th-century mission artifacts. Also visit the mission cemetery, a placid and pretty spot where frontier families and about 4000 Chumash Indians are buried in the shade of a Moreton Bay fig tree. Admission. ~ 2201 Laguna Street; 805-682-4713, fax 805-682-6067; www.sbmission.org.

Farther uphill at the **Santa Barbara Museum of Natural History** are successive rooms devoted to marine, plant, vertebrate, and insect life. Excellent for kids, it also features an extensive collection of artifacts from the local Chumash tribe. You'll recognize the museum by the 72-foot skeleton of a blue whale out front. There is also a lizard lounge and a planetarium with a space lab. Admis-

Mission Santa Barbara.

sion. ~ 2559 Puesta del Sol Road; 805-682-4711, fax 805-569-3170; www.sbnature.org, e-mail info@sbnature2.org.

Nearby Mission Canyon Road continues into the hills for close up views of the rocky Santa Ynez Mountains and a tour of **Santa Barbara Botanic Garden.** Trails here wind past eight different habitats, including a desert section carpeted with cactus and a meadow filled with wildflowers. In the spring, near the top of the garden, beyond the ancient Indian step, where the forest edges down from the mountains, is a stand of cool lofty redwood trees. Be sure to visit the traditional Japanese teahouse and tea garden exhibit. Guided tours daily. Ad-

Mission Rose Garden.

mission. ~ 1212 Mission Canyon Road; 805-682-4726, fax 805-563-0352; www.sbbg.org, e-mail info@sbbg.org.

One of the prettiest views in Santa Barbara is the mission and the foothills as seen across a field of flowering, multicolored roses. The **Mission Park and Rose Garden**, with its large grassy area, bubbling fountain, and a thousand-plus varieties of roses, is a relaxing little park perfect for a picnic or some Frisbee slinging. But were it not for concerned citizens, it could have wound up as a housing complex. When the Franciscans put the property up for sale after the 1925 earthquake, it was saved from development by locals who raised the money to purchase it for the city. ~ Los Olivos and Laguna streets.

PARKS

A trip to 19-acre **Rocky Nook Park** will give you a feel for the landscape before Santa Barbara was even a glimmer in a developer's eye. The land was donated by the friends of a local estate owner, from whom they purchased the property and deeded it to the city. Mature California live oaks, sycamores, and other native trees and plants provide shade for picnics and walks, and spring-fed Mission Creek burbles through the rustic park year-round. ~ 610 Mission Canyon Road; 805-681-5650, 805-568-2459.

In the foothills near the Botanic Gardens, **Skofield Park** has grassy meadows and reservable picnic and barbe-

Green Gem

Designed as a horticultural showplace in 1921, **Orpet Park** is a lush haven tucked in among the spectacular homes on The Riviera. Four acres of exotic plants and trees, ocean views, walking paths, picnic tables, and its proximity to the mission area sights, make this a great place for a picnic lunch. ~ Alameda Padre Serra and Moreno Road; 805-564-5418.

cue sites, but for hikers the attraction is its access to the Rattlesnake Trail. This moderate three-and-a-half-mile roundtrip hike takes you along Rattlesnake Canyon and Mission Creek on a well-maintained trail that, happily for hikers, is off limits to mountain bikers. ~ 1819 Las Canoas Road; 805-564-5418, fax 805-564-5480.

Westside   The Westside, one of Santa Barbara's oldest residential neighborhoods, is where you will find charmingly renovated turn-of-the-city homes, 1920s' California bungalows, and picture perfect B&Bs. In the 1860s the Westside became the city's first Anglo neighborhood; and, although it's currently a quiet residential area, it almost wound up as Hollywood-central. During the 1910s thirteen movie studios called Santa Barbara home including the country's largest company, American Film Manufacturing (or "Flying A"). Located on Mission and State streets, it churned out some of the country's most popular silent films. However, by the early '20s the film industry was traveling south toward more sun and more space—ending Santa Barbara's affair with the silver screen.

LODGING

Simpson House Inn

121 East Arrellaga Street
805-963-7067, 800-676-1280, fax 805-564-4811
www.simpsonhouseinn.com, e-mail info@simpsonhouseinn.com
15 rooms
ULTRA-DELUXE

Small and intimate as bed and breakfasts tend to be, the Simpson House Inn is even more so. Close to downtown, it resides along a quiet tree-lined block secluded in an acre of English gardens complete with fountains and intimate sitting areas. The century-old Victorian inn features 15 guest rooms, restored barn suites, and garden cottages all decorated with antiques and fine art. Some feature private decks or patios, fireplaces, and jacuzzis. A gourmet breakfast is served on the verandah or in private

Enchanting El Encanto

El Encanto Hotel & Garden Villas sits high in the Santa Barbara hills and is a favorite hideaway among Hollywood stars. The hotel's 84 rooms are set in cottages and villas that dot this ten-acre retreat. The grounds are beautifully landscaped and feature a lily pond, a tennis court, and a swimming pool. The views are simply spectacular. Rooms are very spacious with attached sitting rooms, plus extra amenities like room service, a refrigerator, and terrycloth bathrobes. Some have private patios. The decor is French country with a lot of brass and etched glass fixtures. ~ 1900 Lasuen Road; 805-687-5000, 800-346-7039, fax 805-687-3903; www.elencantohotel.com, e-mail yourstay@ elencantohotel.com. ULTRA-DELUXE.

El Encanto boasts a luxurious dining room as well as a terrace for dining outdoors. The views are phenomenal, with all of Santa Barbara rooms or patios; beverages are served in the afternoon, and hors d'oeuvres and wine are provided in the evening. Bikes and croquet round out the package.

The Glenborough Inn
1327 Bath Street
805-966-0589, 800-962-0589
www.glenboroughinn.com, e-mail santabarbara@glenborough
  inn.com
17 rooms
DELUXE TO ULTRA-DELUXE

The Glenborough Inn is laid out in similar fashion to the Simpson House. The main house is a 1906 California craftsman design with extensive wood detailing and period furniture. A suite in the main house is decorated in turn-of-the-20th-century nouveau style with a fireplace, private entrance, garden, and jacuzzi tub. The second house is an 1880s-era cottage with rooms and suites that

stretching below this hillside perch. Dinner is a gourmet experience, featuring imaginative California and French cuisine. Changing weekly according to harvest and catch, the menu might include sautéed sea bass with a tarragon crust, roast tenderloin of beef with garlic mashed potatoes, or angel hair pasta with roasted garlic and organic red and yellow tomatoes. The appetizers and desserts are equally amazing, as are the breakfast and lunch courses. Jackets are required for men at dinner. Open for lunch, dinner, and Sunday brunch. ~ DELUXE TO ULTRA-DELUXE.

A relaxing way to wind down a busy day of sightseeing is to drop by the El Encanto lounge for a drink. Nothing quite compares to watching the city lights flicker on as the sun reaches its last rays over the silvery harbor.

have fireplaces and private baths. The theme in both abodes is romance; they are beautifully fashioned with embroidered curtains, inlaid French furniture, some canopied beds, crocheted coverlets, and needlepoint pieces. Several rooms have jacuzzi tubs. Guests enjoy a gourmet breakfast brought to their door, and nightly tea and cookies; they also share a cozy living room that has a tile fireplace.

Bath Street Inn
1720 Bath Street
805-682-9680, 800-341-2284, fax 805-569-1281
www.bathstreetinn.com, e-mail bathstin@slicom.com
12 rooms
DELUXE TO ULTRA-DELUXE

Down the road at the Bath Street Inn you'll encounter a Queen Anne Victorian constructed in 1890. Enter along a garden walkway into a warm living room with a marble-trimmed fireplace. The patio in back is set in another garden. Some of the guest rooms on the second floor feature the hardwood floors and patterned wallpaper that are the hallmarks of California bed and break-

fasts. The third floor has a cozy sloped roof and a television lounge for guests. Rooms include private baths, televisions, breakfast, and evening refreshments.

The Upham Hotel
1404 De la Vina Street
805-962-0058, 800-727-0876
fax 805-963-2825
www.uphamhotel.com, e-mail upham.hotel@verizon.net
50 rooms
ULTRA-DELUXE

The Upham Hotel is "the oldest cosmopolitan hotel in continuous operation in Southern California." Established in 1871, it shares a sense of history with the country inns, but enjoys the lobby and restaurant amenities of a hotel. Victorian in style, the two-story clapboard is marked by sweeping verandahs and a cupola; the accommodations here are nicely appointed with hardwood and period furnishings. Around the landscaped grounds are garden cottages, some with private patios and fire-

Best Western Encina Lodge & Suites places, and a carriage house with five Victorian-style rooms. Continental breakfast, afternoon wine and cheese, and cookies at bedtime are included.

Best Western Encina Lodge & Suites
2220 Bath Street
805-682-7277, 800-526-2282, fax 805-563-9319
www.bestwestern.com
121 rooms
MODERATE

The Best Western Encina Lodge & Suites, with its balconies and brightly colored flowers, feels more like a Swiss chalet than a remodeled 1950s motel. Some thought has gone into making the rooms resemble the individualistic B&B style, rather than the more sterile room decor typical of most ersatz downtown motels. There's a pool and spa, and special touches, which include fruit and cookies in the room upon arrival, and a massage service that will, for a fee, send a masseuse to your room.

Secret Garden Inn & Cottages

1908 Bath Street
805-687-2300, fax 805-687-4576
www.secretgarden.com, e-mail garden@secretgarden.com
11 rooms
MODERATE TO DELUXE

Secret Garden Inn & Cottages is a neat and tidy wood-frame house tucked in among lush plantings. Gardens, patios, and pathways add to the lovely setting. Built in 1905 to accommodate a large family, most rooms are decorated in a minimally ruffled feminine style using pastel colors and flowered fabrics and wallpaper. All the cottage accommodations have private entrances, some with decks. On a nice morning the generous breakfast buffet, which includes quiche, fruit, and fresh-baked muffins and scones, can be enjoyed on a tree-shaded patio.

Tiffany Country House

1323 De la Vina Street
805-963-2283, 800-999-5672, fax 805-963-2825
www.tiffanycountryhouse.com, e-mail frontdesk@tiffanycountry
     house.com
7 rooms
DELUXE

PICTURE-PERFECT
B&Bs

1. **Tiffany Country House,** *p. 123*
2. **Cheshire Cat Inn,** *p. 125*
3. **Bath Street Inn,** *p. 120*
4. **Secret Garden Inn & Cottages,**
   p. 123

Tiffany Country House looks much as it must of at the turn of the 20th century when it was a two-story family residence. This unpretentious big white wooden house has a charming third-story dormer room and many of its original features, including hardwood floors and leaded glass windows. Each of the seven rooms are individually decorated in a sophisticated country style, with interesting art and antiques befitting the room's character. All come with private baths, ceiling fans, comfy upholstered chairs, and beds with either iron or interesting wooden headboards. Some rooms also have wood-burning fireplaces and whirlpool tubs. Hot breakfast in the morning and wine and cheese in the evening can be enjoyed in the garden or around the living room fireplace.

Bayberry Inn
I I I West Valerio Street
805-569-3398, fax 805-569-1120
www.bayberryinnsantabarbara.com, e-mail info@bayberryinnsanta
    barbara.com
8 rooms
DELUXE

Designated a Structure of Merit by the Santa Barbara Landmarks Commission, the American Colonial–style Bayberry Inn has been everything from a private residence to a sorority house, until the 1980s when it became a B&B. All the rooms have queen-sized canopy beds, private baths, individual color schemes, and are adorned with fresh cut flowers from a neighboring garden. In the morning a full breakfast is served on the garden deck, coffee, tea, and hot chocolate are available all day, and at night a yummy homemade dessert appears. You can even indulge in a rousing game of English croquet on the manicured lawn.

Cheshire Cat Inn
36 West Valerio Street
805-569-1610, fax 805-682-1876
www.cheshirecat.com, e-mail cheshire@cheshirecat.com
21 rooms
DELUXE

The Cheshire Cat Inn, housed in one of Santa Barbara's most elegant and well-restored Queen Anne Victorians, was one of Santa Barbara's first luxury B&Bs. Appropriate to its exterior, the inn is decorated in Laura Ashley fabrics and English antiques. Accommodations include individual rooms, cottages, and suites, with amenities that may include jacuzzis, balconies, hot tubs, and

A Cup or a Cone?

For an over-the-top ice cream fix, and to hell with the carbs, calories, and cholesterol, nothing beats **McConnell's Fine Ice Creams**. This home-grown Santa Barbara business has been churning out sinfully rich ice cream  since 1949. Originally the company sold all of its ice cream out of a building on the corner of Mission and State streets. Today McConnell's can be found in upscale grocery stores and restaurants and in their ice cream shop down the street from the original location. What sets McConnell's apart is the ingredients. Fresh cream comes from local dairies, vanillas are made specially for the company, eggs are locally produced, and cocoas come from Guittard in San Francisco. No artificial ingredients or stabilizers are ever used and the flavors, running the gamut from Dutch chocolate to Russian Nesselrode, are varied and creamily dreamy. ~ 201 West Mission Street; 805-569-2323, fax 805-965-3764; www.mcconnells.com.

---

fireplaces. Breakfast, afternoon refreshments, and evening wine and hors d'oeuvres are all included in the room rate. The inn also has two spa therapy rooms on the property with trained therapists who can massage the aches away either here or in your room.

Eastside
During the 1890s the Eastside of Santa Barbara was developing a radical divide between wealthy homes on the upper Eastside and the working-class neighborhood of the lower Eastside. Today in and around the lower Eastside's main commercial thoroughfare of Milpas Street, a substantial portion of the city's Latino population live and shop. The area is a perfect spot to cruise

corner stores and dine at the city's best Mexican restaurants. The upper Eastside, bordering the Mission District, has embraced its opposing side's diversity, though it still maintains its historic elegance with some early-20th-century mansions, cottages, and bungalows.

DINING

La Tolteca
616 East Haley Street
805-963-0847, fax 805-963-3057
breakfast, lunch, and dinner
BUDGET

Best of Santa Barbara's low-priced restaurants is La Tolteca, not to be confused with La Tolteca Restaurant on Milpas Street. This self-order café serves delicious Mexican food. Everything is fresh, making it the place for tacos, tostadas, burritos, tamales, and enchiladas. Menu items are served à la carte, so you can mix and match to get exactly what you want. You can sit at one of the few tables inside or out near the sidewalk.

Piñatas on Milpas Street.

La Super Rica

622 North Milpas Street
805-963-4940
BUDGET

One of the Eastside's south-of-the-border favorites is La Super Rica. Along with traditional fare such as chiles rellenos, the menu includes *alambre de pechuga* (marinated chicken strips fried with peppers and onions on a warm tortilla). The homemade salsa is outstanding and, best yet, they press their tortillas right there. Just be prepared for a line.

Shang Hai

830 North Milpas Street
805-962-7833
no lunch on Sunday; closed Tuesday
BUDGET

Don't expect ambience and charm, just decent Chinese food at reasonable prices. Hidden away in a Milpas Street strip mall, Shang Hai is a great place for a vegetarian meal. Tofu is substituted in the usual beef,

HIDDEN

The Well-Heeled Cowboy (and Girl)

Jedlicka's, which started out as a shoe repair and bookmaking business in the 1930s, has for years been the premier place in Santa Barbara to go for western wear and horse-related items. Catering to both riders and their horses, Jedlicka's is filled with boots in every color and style. There are over 4000 pairs of western jeans, 900 Stetsons, and 140 styles of hats, as well as saddles and bridles. ~ 2605 De la Vina Street; 805-687-0747, 800-681-0747; www.jedlickas.com.

Salsa Alert

In an atmosphere reminiscent of casual restaurants south of the border, **Julian's Mexican Cafe** serves some of the freshest and best Mexican food in town. The food transcends the usual stateside Mexican fare, with specialties like *adobada* tacos (made with thin strips of grilled vinegar-dipped pork marinated in chile sauce) and *sopes* (home-made corn cups topped with beans and grilled vegetables). But be forewarned, the green tomatillo salsa is addicting. ~ 421 North Milpas Street; 805-564-2322. BUDGET.

chicken, and shrimp dishes, making the fare lighter and less filling. And even if tofu doesn't get your heart racing, you'd almost swear that the vegetarian beef in black bean sauce was made with fantastically tender beef rather than the humble soy bean.

Your Place
22-A North Milpas Street
phone/fax 805-966-5151
closed Monday
BUDGET

Your Place is a favorite with locals and the place to satisfy a craving for spicy Thai food in a no-frills atmosphere. Dishes in this little restaurant are prepared to whatever degree of hotness your palate can tolerate, be it mild, medium, hot, or "call the fire department." Specialties include pineapple fried rice (fried pineapple with shrimp, chicken, cashew nuts, and rice served in a pineapple shell) and *kah kai* soup (hot and sour soup

with chicken, coconut milk and *galanga* served in a flaming hot pot). Cool off the effects of the searing chiles with a cold Singha beer.

Hope Ranch
One hardly needs the elegant sign that towers over Las Palmas Drive to know that this is the entrance to exclusive commercial-free Hope Ranch. Here the coastal route winds into dense foliage, the rustic backdrop for the multimillion dollar villas and mansions composing Santa Barbara's most secluded enclave. A spectacular golf course loops around the lagoon at the center of Hope Ranch, while the forested areas farther toward the sea hold rugged equestrian paths that cross the twisting roads. On the surface Hope Ranch appears to be solely about seclusion and country clubs. However, as you look a little deeper, it's easy to notice the unrivaled tranquility that has drawn so many people to settle here.

Montecito
Despite its name, "Little Mountain," you'd be challenged to find anything minuscule about

Montecito, a community that flanks Santa Barbara to the south. During the 18th century the area amounted to a small Chumash village and a hundred years later it was mostly orchards and farms. But by the 1900s it began to become what it is today, a neighborhood for the wealthy, with lush landscapes hiding gated mansions and designer homes. This is the place for high-end boutique shopping, tony restaurants, and top-of-the-line hotels.

SIGHTS

One former resident, Madame Ganna Walska, turned her hillside estate into what is now one of the most famous private gardens in the country: **Lotusland**. By the time she arrived in Santa Barbara in 1941, Madame, a Polish-born opera singer, was on her sixth husband. He persuaded her to buy a Montecito estate in order to establish a spiritual center for Tibetan scholar-monks. When

Japanese garden at Lotusland.

that idea, along with the marriage, failed, Madame turned to horticulture. The result was a magnificent private garden that visitors may tour on a reservations-only basis. The gardens are closed Sunday through Tuesday and mid-November to mid-February. Admission. ~ 805-969-9990, fax 805-969-4423; www.lotusland.org, e-mail info@lotusland.org.

After exploring the town's shady groves and manicured lawns, you can pick up **Channel Drive**, a spectacular street that skirts beaches and bluffs as it loops back toward Santa Barbara. From this curving roadway you'll spy oddly shaped structures offshore. Looking like a line of battleships ready to attack Santa Barbara, they are in fact **oil derricks**. Despite protests from environmentalists and

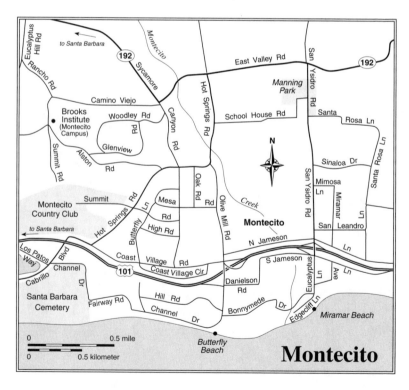

a disastrous 1969 oil spill, these coastal waters have been the site of drilling operations for decades. Those hazy humps farther out past the wells are the Channel Islands.

LODGING

Four Seasons Biltmore Hotel

1260 Channel Drive
805-969-2261, 800-332-3442, fax 805-565-8323
www.fourseasons.com
213 rooms
ULTRA-DELUXE

Santa Barbara's two finest hotels dominate the town's two geographic locales, the ocean and the mountains. Four Seasons Biltmore Hotel is a grand old Spanish-style hotel set on 20 acres beside the beach. It's the kind of place where guests play croquet or practice putting on manicured lawns, then meander over to the hotel's Coral Casino Beach and Cabana Club. There are several dining rooms

Four Seasons Biltmore Hotel.

as well as tennis courts, swimming pools, and a complete spa. The refurbished rooms are quite large and have an airy feel, with light wood furnishings and full marble baths. Many are located in multiplex cottages and are spotted around the magnificent grounds that have made this one of California's most famous hotels since it opened back in 1927.

San Ysidro Ranch

900 San Ysidro Lane
805-969-5046, 800-368-6788, fax 805-565-1995
www.sanysidroranch.com
38 rooms
ULTRA-DELUXE

In the Santa Ynez foothills above Montecito sits another retreat where the rich and powerful mix with the merely talented. San Ysidro Ranch sprawls across 500 acres, most of which is wilderness traversed by hiking trails. There are tennis courts, a pool, a bocce ball court, and complete fitness facilities. The grounds vie with the Santa Barbara Botanic Garden in the variety of plant life: there are meadows, mountain forests, and an orange grove. The Stonehouse Restaurant serves gourmet dishes and the complex also features sit-

Resident Connoisseur

Long before the Food Network came along, Julia Child revolutionized American cooking. She made gourmet recipes accessible to all on television's first-ever cooking show, "The French Chef," which debuted February 11, 1963. A native Californian, Child owned a place in an upscale Montecito retirement community, where she passed away in 2004 at age 91. When in town, the 6-foot 2-inch Child cut an unmistakable figure at Santa Barbara's Saturday Farmer's Market. She also took an avid interest in the careers of local chefs and enjoyed calling them out of the kitchen when a particular meal pleased her. Despite her gourmet status, Child was never a food snob; in fact, her favorite Mexican restaurant was Eastside's La Super Rica.

ting rooms and lounges. Privacy is the password: all these *Butterfly* features are shared by guests occupying just 38 units. The *Beach.* accommodations are dotted around the property in cottages and small multiplexes. Pets are welcome; 24-hour room service is available. Rooms vary in decor, but even the simplest are trimly appointed and spacious with hardwood furnishings, wood-burning fireplaces, king-sized beds, and a mountain, ocean, or garden view. Many have hot tubs.

Montecito Inn

1295 Coast Village Road
805-969-7854, 800-843-2017, fax 805-969-0623
www.montecitoinn.com, e-mail info@montecitoinn.com
61 rooms
DELUXE TO ULTRA-DELUXE

In the 1920s silent-screen legend Charlie Chaplin had the Montecito Inn built to accommodate both him and his Hollywood friends on their frequent visits to Santa Barbara. Reminiscent of a European boutique ho-

Text continued on page 138.

Coast Village Road

Montecito's Coast Village Road is where the rich and famous shop. This broad thoroughfare, with its eucalyptus-planted center divider, is lined with businesses, restaurants, and hotels. Even if you can't afford the steep prices in the various high-end boutiques, art galleries, and antique stores, it's fun to look and imagine what you might buy if you had an over-the-top bank account.

After lunch at the Montecito Café head west and stop at **Saffron** for a look at the unique woman's wear and

Asian-influenced art objects. ~ 1275 Coast Village Road; 805-565-9596.

For a cool interlude among the most beautiful of plants and flowers, look for an opening through the towering hedge and you'll find yourself in the lush wonderland that is **Turk Hessellund Nursery**. ~ 1255 Coast Village Road; 805-969-5871.

Lily specializes in home furnishings in earthy tones and natural woods and fibers. Everything from patio furniture and umbrellas to accent pieces are un-

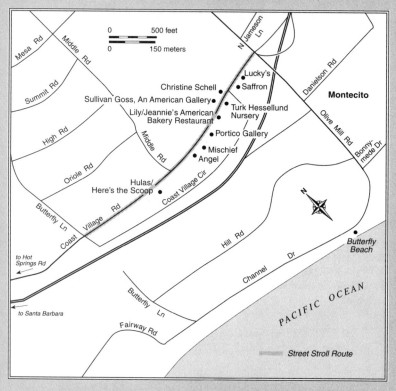

derstatedly expensive looking. ~ 1253 Coast Village Road; 805-695-0625.

If an after-lunch coffee sounds appealing, stop by **Jeannie's American Bakery Restaurant**. If there's a table available on the deck overlooking the sidewalk, sit a spell and watch the passing parade. ~ 1253 Coast Village Road; 805-969-7878.

Portico Gallery specializes in paintings and sculpture by contemporary national and California artists. Besides walls full of salable art, Portico offers ongoing art classes for all ages and levels right in the gallery. ~ 1235 Coast Village Road; 805-695-8850.

Mischief is the place to go for diaphanous women's clothing with individual flair. ~ 1225 Coast Village Road; 805-565-9588. Just down the street at **Angel**, hip designs appeal to young mothers and socialites. ~ 1221 Coast Village Road; 805-565-3120. And for more casual, and certainly less expensive, clothing, **Hulas** carries Hawaiian-type garb for the beachy set. ~ 1187 Coast Village Road #5; 805-969-6926.

If all of this high-toned shopping, be it actual or window only, has worked up an appetite, stop in at **Here's the Scoop** for a gelato. A homegrown business, this ice cream parlor makes all of its gelatos on the premises, and the flavor selections are impressive, including everything from one using local strawberries to cinnamon. ~ 1187 Coast Village Road (lower level); 805-969-7020.

At this point cross the street and start back. Across from the Montecito Inn, at **Sullivan Goss, An American Gallery**, the emphasis is on California landscape paintings both old and new by some of the state's foremost painters, while featured artists are showcased in various special exhibitions during the year. ~ 1266 Coast Village Road; 805-969-5112.

Next step into **Christine Schell** and check out the fine antiques and other beautiful objects that are likely to eventually adorn a Montecito mansion. ~ 1268 Coast Village Road; 805-565-4859.

Cross the street again and you're back where you started, perhaps in time for a frosty martini and some people watching at the bar at **Lucky's**. ~ 1279 Coast Village Road; 805-565-7540.

The Right Prescription

One of the first businesses to be built in what is now known as Montecito Village, the **San Ysidro Pharmacy** is a drug store, gift shop, and coffeehouse. But it's the tables on the front patio overlooking San Ysidro and East Valley roads that are coveted by breakfasting and lunching locals. Jonathan Winters has been spotted here wisecracking over morning coffee, and there's almost no place better to get a feel for the rich and relaxed lifestyle of one of California's toniest communities. Breakfast and lunch only. Closed Sunday. ~ 1498 East Valley Road; 805-969-2284. BUDGET TO MODERATE.

tel, most of the rooms are on the small side, but beautifully and individually decorated in warm earth tones with handpainted ceramic tile accents in the bathrooms. The elevator is original, with iron gates and room for, at the most, two people with luggage. In the Italian marble-adorned lobby guests can eat the free continental breakfast cozied up to a glowing fireplace.

DINING

Lucky's
1279 Coast Village Road
805-565-7540
weekend brunch
ULTRA-DELUXE

A chic New York–style restaurant, Lucky's is currently Montecito's in spot. This is the place where Santa Barbara's wealthy and famous sip perfectly dry martinis and dine on the finest beef available surrounded by black-and-white photographs of Hollywood screen legends. Though they have fresh seafood, the real reason to come here is for the red meat. Even the hamburger is a step above, and the aged New York steak practically melts in your mouth. Perfection doesn't come cheap, but for a special occasion the excellent food and service make it worth the splurge.

Montecito Café
1295 Coast Village Road
805-969-3392
MODERATE

Bright and airy, with plenty of windows looking out to Coast Village Road, the Montecito Café is popular with locals looking for good food at fair prices. Located off the lobby of the Montecito Inn, tables in the front room surround a burbling tiled fountain. Specializing in light and creative entrées, salads, and sandwiches, and featuring local wines, the restaurant is almost always filled. Some of the favorites include the fresh-fish-of-the-

Montecito firehouse weathervane.

day sandwich with fries, New York pepper steak with sundried tomatoes, and sky-high coconut cake.

SHOPPING

For years, **Tecolote Book Shop** has reigned as Montecito's only independent bookstore. The difference between Tecolote and most neighborhood bookshops, however, is that it's not unusual for bestsellers to be written by locals such as Sue Grafton and Oprah Winfrey. Facing the grassy area of Montecito Village, this cozy store is a good place to go for books on local places and has a well-stocked children's section. ~ 1470 East Valley Road; 805-969-4977.

When **Pierre LaFond** opened his store in 1964 it consisted of a large liquor department and a gift shop that specialized in items from around the world. Today the focus is on gourmet take-out and fine wines. Sweet freaks can get a sugar rush just by stepping into the candy and ice cream room, while java lovers can order fancy coffee drinks, accompanied by freshly made scones and pastries. Everything from individual quiches to chicken Caesar salad sandwiches are available at the deli counter, and you can leisurely enjoy your food and drink of choice while watching the world go by at one of the outside tables. ~ 516 San Ysidro Road; 805-565-1502; www.pierrelafond.com.

For anyone who loves fine bedding **Baroncelli Linen** is heaven. The highest tread counts and most luxuriously feeling sheets and pillow cases are the norm in this little shop catering to linen lovers with large bank accounts. ~ 1485 East Valley Road, Suite 8; 805-969-2617.

HIDDEN

Miramar Beach

Miramar Beach was so named for the hotel that fronted it for more than a century. With the property now being in a state of flux, the beach must be accessed from the end of Eucalyptus Lane. Broad and sandy, this is a great beach for walking, particularly when the tide is out and you can walk to Summerland Beach in the east or connect up with Butterfly Beach to the west. Low tide is also a good time to uncover sea creatures sheltered in rocky tidepools.

NIGHTLIFE

La Sala is the elegant lobby lounge at the Four Seasons Biltmore, where live music and dancing (the kind in which couples actually hold each other in their arms) have become very popular on Friday and Saturday nights. The music varies nightly. ~ 1260 Channel Drive, Santa Barbara; 805-969-2261, 800-332-3442.

BEACHES & PARKS

A lovely stretch of beach across from the Four Seasons Biltmore, **Butterfly Beach** is the most west-facing of Santa Barbara's beaches, making it the best beach for sunset-over-the-water viewing. Beach ac-

cess is easy, thanks to periodic short flights of stairs, and if you arrive early there is convenient parking along Channel Drive. When the tide's out you can walk for miles both east and west. ~ Channel Drive.

In the 1930s the Manning family donated their prime Montecito property to the city to use as a public park. Tucked away in a neighborhood of multi-million dollar homes, **Manning Park** remains a peaceful lushly landscaped haven. Just down the street from Montecito Village, this is the perfect hidden spot to savor a gourmet picnic lunch from Pierre LaFond's at one of the picnic tables or on a tree-shaded bench. ~ 449 San Ysidro Road; 805-969-0201.

5.

South of Santa Barbara

South of Santa Barbara the Central Coast stretches along the Pacific into the valleys, as the rocky shores of the Channel Islands draw closer to the mainland. Summerland, the first community south of Santa Barbara, boasts hillside houses and a tiny main street filled with a hodge-podge of mom-and-pop businesses.

In its early days as a town, neighboring Carpinteria was an expanse of ranch lands and farming communities. As the ranches gave way to housing developments Carpinteria became what it is today, a bedroom community housing commuters for nearby Santa Barbara.

Farther inland the spectacular drive down Highway 150 hints of how the area looked when citrus and avocado ranches dominated the area; sprawling hillside ranches stud the trip into the Ojai Valley.

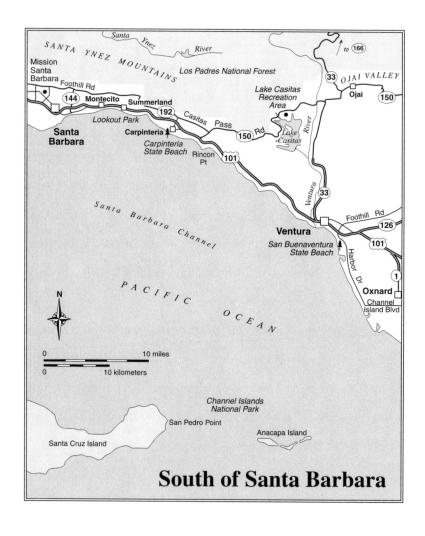

South of Santa Barbara

The town of Ojai itself is an upscale rural town that appeals to artists and mystics. Shops filled with original art, state-of-the-art spas and tony eateries occupy streets and properties shaded by California live oaks and other native trees and plants. A nine-mile bike path runs from Foster Park near Ventura to Ojai Village and is a great way to see the area at a leisurely pace.

Backtracking onto Route 101 you'll find Ventura, a working town with history. Its small but lovely mission and other historic buildings share the main street with myriad antique and collectables shops. In addition, the city is the primary gateway to the Channel Islands. Once the exclusive domain of the Chumash Indians, the islands are home to flora and fauna found nowhere else. Today these commercial-free volcanic outcroppings are visited mostly by backpackers, hikers, kayakers, birders, and day-trippers.

Summerland and Carpinteria
Beginning just south of Santa Barbara, spread out over the hills below Montecito is the small village of Summerland, founded by rancher and supernatural aficionado Harry L. Williams in late 19th century. Fittingly, Williams' personal residence, now the town's most visible landmark, **The Big Yellow House**, is rumored to be haunted, and the main street is lined with antique stores, nurseries, and restaurants.

Five minutes south of Summerland on the ocean side of the 101 sits Carpinteria. Many travelers are barely aware of its existence, but in contrast to its more high-profile neighbors, this is a low-key working community with one of the area's safest beaches and plenty of antique and thrift shops for browsing.

LODGING

Inn on Summer Hill

2520 Lillie Avenue, Summerland
805-969-9998, 800-845-5566, fax 805-565-9946
www.innonsummerhill.com, e-mail info@innonsummerhill.com
17 rooms
ULTRA-DELUXE

The 17 cozy rooms overlooking the Pacific that make up the Inn on Summer Hill have one major drawback—the small stretch of land separating the inn from the sea is sliced by Route 101 and the coast railway. The inn itself makes up for its mediocre location by offering first-rate accommodations and amenities that include fireplaces, king-sized beds with down comforters, whirlpool tubs, and hardwood floors. If you can stand the noisy neighbors you'll find the inn to be the best Summerland has to offer.

Prufrock's Garden Inn by the Beach

600 Linden Avenue, Carpinteria
805-566-9696, 877-837-6257, fax 805-566-9404
www.prufrocks.com, e-mail reservations@prufrocks.com
8 rooms
DELUXE TO ULTRA-DELUXE

Prufrocks Garden Inn is the intimate bed and breakfast straddling Carpinteria's main drag of Linden Avenue and the local beach park. Caretakers Jim and Judy Halvorsen have transformed this rickety old house into a wonderful inn featuring eight quiet rooms, a country-style sitting room and adjoining garden. Open year-round, the inn offers guests home-cooked breakfast daily and hors d'oeuvres in the evening.

DINING

The Nugget

2318 Lillie Avenue, Summerland
805-969-6135
BUDGET TO MODERATE

With its western false front and game trophies adorning the dining room walls along with grainy black-and-white-photos of California's rugged cowboy past, you may not think The Nugget Restaurant belongs on the sunbaked coast. But this is a restaurant with a unique style, where you order steak, chicken, and fresh fish from a 19th-century newspaper menu, and although the ocean sits just yards away you'll begin to feel the fit of the Old West.

The Palms

701 Linden Avenue, Carpinteria
805-684-3811, fax 805-684-2149
dinner only
BUDGET TO DELUXE

One of Carpinteria's favorite hangouts for locals and visitors is The Palms restaurant. Situated in the heart of town, The Palms welcomes you to grill up your own steak or order fresh seafood and other American specialties. The restaurant is only open for dinner but the cocktail lounge is one of the city's most popular spots, featuring live music on the weekends.

Clementine's Steak House

4631 Carpinteria Avenue, Carpinteria
phone/fax 805-684-5119
dinner only, closed Monday
MODERATE TO DELUXE

A step upscale, Clementine's Steak House features filet mignon, fresh fish dishes, vegetarian casserole, steak teriyaki, and Danish-style liver. It's dinner only here, but the meal—which includes soup, salad, vegetable, side dish, homemade bread, and pie—could hold you well into the next day. The interior has a beamed ceiling and patterned wallpaper. Lean back in a captain's chair and enjoy some home-style cooking.

BEACHES

Part of the narrow strip of white sand composing **Summerland Beach** used to be a popular nude beach. It's backed by low-lying hills, which afford privacy from the nearby freeway and railroad tracks. The favored skinny-dipping spot is on the east end between two protective rock piles. Gay men sometimes congregate farther down the beach at **Loon Point**, but families are rapidly taking over. Nudists beware: law enforcement at the beach has

PICTURE-PERFECT
Nature Adventures

1. **Hiking on Anacapa Island,** *p. 155*
2. **Birdwatching on Santa Cruz Island,** *p. 154*
3. **Bicycling through Ojai,** *p. 162*

been stepped up in response to public demand. There are no facilities here, but nearby **Lookout Park** (805-969-1720) has picnic areas, restrooms, and a playground. Swimming is popular, and there is good bodysurfing here. ~ Located in Summerland six miles east of Santa Barbara. Take the Summerland exit off Route 101 and get on Wallace Avenue, the frontage road between the freeway and ocean. Follow it east for three-tenths of a mile to Finney Road and the beach.

Rincon Beach County Park, wildly popular with nudists and surfers, is a pretty, white-sand beach backed by bluffs. At the bottom of the wooden stairway leading down to the beach, take a right along the strand and head over to the seawall. There will often be a bevy of nude sunbathers snuggled here between the hillside and the ocean in an area known as Bates Beach, or Backside Rincon. Be warned: Nude sunbathing is illegal. Occasionally the sheriff will crack down on those in the buff. Surfers, on the other hand, should turn left and paddle

out to Rincon Point, one of the most popular surfing spots along the entire California coast. There are picnic areas and restrooms. ~ Located three miles southeast of Carpinteria; from Route 101 take the Bates Road exit.

The ribbon-shaped park that extends for nearly a mile along the coast of Carpinteria is simply known as **Carpinteria State Beach**. Bordered to the east by dunes and along the west by a bluff, the beach has an offshore shelf that shelters it from the surf. As a result, Carpinteria provides exceptionally good swimming and is nicknamed "the world's safest beach." Wildlife here consists of small mammals and reptiles as well as seals and many seabirds. Don't bring your pets; dogs are not allowed on the beach. It's a good spot for tidepooling; there is also a lagoon here. The Santa Ynez Mountains rise in the background. Facilities include picnic areas, restrooms, dressing rooms, showers, and lifeguards (during summer only). Swimming is excellent, and skindiving is good along the breakwater reef, a habitat for abalone and lobsters. Surfing is very good in the "tar pits" area near the east end of the park. If you are into fishing, cabezon, corbina, and barred perch are caught here. Day-use fee, $8. ~ Located at the end of Palm Avenue in Carpinteria; 805-684-2811.

Camping: There are 261 tent/RV sites, about half with hookups, from $21 to $39 per night. Reservations: 800-444-7275.

The Channel Islands

Gaze out from the Ventura or Santa Barbara shoreline and you will spy a fleet of islands moored offshore. At times fringed with mist, on other occasions standing a hand's reach away in the crystal air, they are the Channel Islands, a group of eight volcanic islands.

Situated in the Santa Barbara Channel, 11 to 60 miles from the coast, they are a place apart, a wild and storm-blown region of sharp cliffs, rocky coves, and curving grasslands. Five of the islands—Anacapa, Santa Cruz, Santa Rosa, San Miguel, and Santa Barbara—comprise Channel Islands National Park while the surrounding waters are a marine sanctuary.

Nicknamed "North America's Galápagos," the chain teems with every imaginable form of life. Sea lions and harbor seals frequent the caves, blowholes, and offshore pillars. Brown pelicans and black oystercatchers roost on the sea arches and sandy beaches. There are tidepools crowded with brilliant purple hydrocorals and white-plumed sea anemones. Like the Galápagos, this isolated archipelago has given rise to many unique life-forms, including over 40 endemic plant species and the island fox, which grows only to the size of a house cat.

The northern islands were created about 30 million years ago by volcanic activity. Archaeological discoveries indicate that they could be among the oldest sites of human habitation in the Americas. When explorer Juan Rodríquez Cabrillo revealed them to Europe in 1542 they were populated with thousands of Chumash Indians.

Today, long since the Chumash were removed and the islands given over to hunters, ranchers, and settlers,

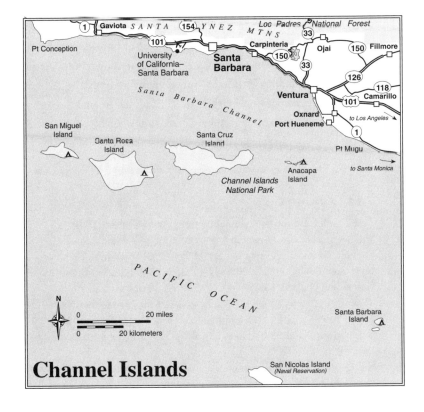

Channel Islands

the Channel Islands are largely uninhabited. All five, however, are open to hikers and campers. At the mainland-based Channel Islands National Park Visitors Center there are contemporary museum displays, an observation deck, an indoor tidepool, and an excellent 23-minute movie to familiarize you with the park. Also on display is a skeleton of a pygmy mammoth found on Santa Rosa Island in 1994. ~ 1901 Spinnaker Drive, Ventura; 805-658-5730, fax 805-658-5799; www.nps.gov/chis.

Santa Cruz Island is the largest and most diverse of the islands. Here you will find an island just 24 miles long that supports 600 species of plants, 130 types of land birds, and several unique plant species. There are Indian middens, earthquake faults, and two mountain ranges to explore. To the center lies a pastoral valley while the shoreline is a rugged region of cliffs, tidepools, and offshore rocks. Note: Camping is not allowed on Nature Conservancy property but is permitted on the eastern part on national park land. Call ahead to make reservations. ~ 1691 Spinnaker Drive, Ventura; 805-642-1393; www.islandpackers.com.

Island Bound

The best access to the Channel Islands is from Ventura. **Island Packers** schedules regular day trips by boat to Anacapa, Santa Barbara, Santa Cruz, Santa Rosa, and San Miguel islands. ~ 1691 Spinnaker Drive, Ventura, 805-642-1393, and 3600 South Harbor Boulevard, Oxnard, 805-382-1779; www.islandpackers.com.
Channel Islands Aviation will fly you to Santa Rosa Island for a day of fishing or hiking or overnight camping. Flights leave at 9 a.m. and return around 3:30 p.m. ~ 805-987-1301; www.flycia.com.

Anacapa Island, the island closest to shore, is a series of three islets parked 11 miles southwest of Oxnard. There is a nature trail here. Like the other islands, it is a prime whale-watching spot and is surrounded by the giant kelp forests that make the Channel Islands one of the nation's richest marine environments.

The varied landscape of **Santa Rosa Island** includes grasslands, volcanic formations, and marshes. You may spot harbor and elephant seals as you stroll the island's beaches. Nature and history draw visitors to **San Miguel Island**, where you can hike to the caliche forest or visit a monument to Juan Cabrillo, the first European to discover California. **Santa Barbara Island** is a good spot for birdwatching. Hikers can traverse the five and a half miles of trails here.

Outdoor aficionados will be glad to hear that camping is allowed in the national park. However, you must ob-

tain a permit by calling 800-365-2267. All campgrounds have picnic tables and pit toilets, but generally, water must be carried in—and trash must be carried out. Fires are not permitted.

Whether you are a sailor, swimmer, day-tripper, hiker, archaeologist, birdwatcher, camper, tidepooler, scuba diver, seal lover, or simply an interested observer, you'll find this amazing island chain a place of singular beauty and serenity.

Ojai   To Chumash Indians the word *ojai* signified the nest. And to the generations of mystics, health aficionados, artists, and admirers who have settled here, the place is indeed a secluded abode. Geographically it resembles its Chumash namesake, nestling in a moon-shaped valley girded by the Topa Topa and Sulphur Mountains.

A town of 7900 souls, Ojai is an artist colony crowded with galleries and studios. The site is also a

Pastoral Pathway

An excellent Ojai sightseeing jaunt follows **Route 150** west as it snakes down from the hills. The valleys are covered with scrub growth and small farms and the heights support lofty forests. The road skirts Lake Casitas, whose 60-mile shoreline is a labyrinth of coves and inlets. This is a lovely spot for biking, birdwatching, or fishing. Ten miles from Ojai the road joins Route 192, which leads to Santa Barbara. This meandering country road, in the hills above Carpinteria, traverses pretty pastureland. All around lies a quiltwork of orchards, fields, and tilled plots. Shade trees overhang the road and horses graze in the distance.

haven for the health conscious, with spas and hot springs. To the metaphysically minded it is a center for several esoteric sects.

Ever since the 1870s, when author Charles Nordhoff publicized the place as a tourist spot, it has been popular with all sorts of visitors. The cultural life of the town focuses around a series of annual music festivals that runs from May to October and range in style from classical to country-and-western to blues. For sport there is nearby Lake Casitas, Los Padres National Forest, 4500-foot mountains, and a 400-mile network of hiking trails.

Inland just 14 miles from Ventura, Ojai is a valley so extraordinary it was used as the setting for Shangri-La in the movie *Lost Horizon* (1937). Sun-bronzed mountains rise in all directions, fields of wildflowers run to the verge

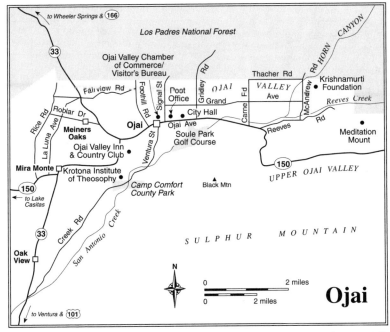

Text continued on page 160.

STREET STROLL
Walk Ventura

Situated 60 miles northwest of Los Angeles and 30 miles to the southeast of Santa Barbara, the 18th-century mission town of Ventura has generally been overlooked by travelers. History has not been so remiss. Long known to the Chumash Indians, who inhabited a nearby village named Shisholop, the place was revealed to Europeans in 1542 by the Portuguese explorer Juan Rodríguez Cabrillo. Father Junípero Serra founded a mission here in 1782 and the region soon became renowned for its fruit orchards.

Today Ventura preserves its heritage in a number of historic sites. Stop by the **Ventura Visitors and Convention Bureau** for brochures and maps. ~ 89 South California Street, Suite C, Ventura; 805-648-2075, 800-333-2989; www.ventura-usa.com, e-mail tourism@ventura-usa.com.

Downtown Ventura is compact and very accessible by foot. The highlight of a stroll through Ventura is **San Buenaventura Mission**. Built in 1782, it stands as the last mission to be founded by Padre Junípero Serra. The whitewash

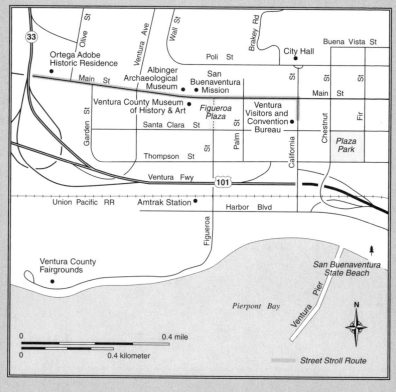

and red-tiled church is flanked by a flowering garden and an elegantly stacked bell tower. Inside, the dark deep chapel is lined with **Stations of the Cross** paintings and features a Romanesque altar adorned with statues and pilasters. My favorite spot is the adjacent garden, a lovely spot with its tile fountain and stately Norfolk pines. Entrance to the mission is actually through a small gift shop a few steps to the east. Admission is $1. ~ 211 East Main Street, Ventura; 805-643-4318; www.sanbuena venturamission.org, e-mail mission@san buenaventuramission.org.

After stopping at the mission, cross Main Street to the **Ventura County Museum of History and Art**, which traces the region's secular history with displays of Chumash Indian artifacts and a farm implement collection. The art gallery features revolving exhibits of local painters and photographers. There's a collection of 32,000 photos depicting Ventura County from its origin to the present day. One gallery features a permanent display of George Stuart's historical figures. The artist is exacting in his detail, right down to the eyelashes and fingernails, when crafting Martin Luther King, Jr., and Abraham Lincoln. A public library and archive houses maps, manuscripts, and photographs pertaining to Ventura County. Closed Monday. Admission. ~ 100 East Main Street, Ventura; 805-653-0323, fax 805-653-5267; www.vcmha.org.

Just west of the mission, the **Albinger Archaeological Museum** sits at the site of an archaeological dig that dates back 3500 years, representing five different native cultures. The small museum displays arrowheads, shell beads, crucifixes, and pottery uncovered here. At the dig site itself you'll see the foundation of an 18th-century mission church, an ancient earth oven, and a remnant of the Spanish padres' elaborate aqueduct system. Closed Monday and Tuesday. ~ 113 East Main Street, Ventura; 805-648-5823, fax 805-653-5267.

Continue west from the museum, about four blocks beyond the mission, to find the **Ortega Adobe Historic Residence**, a small squat home built in 1857 that eventually gave birth to Ortega Chile. With wood-plank furniture and bare interior the home provides a strong example of how hard and rudimentary life was in that early era. Closed Monday and Tuesday. ~ 215 West Main Street, Ventura; 805-658-4726, fax 805-648-1030.

Finally, backtracking toward the San Buenaventura Mission you'll find **Figueroa Plaza**, as you wander down the broad promenade decorated with tile fountains and flowerbeds. This is the site of the town's old Chinatown section, long since faded into history. Only faint remains, such as the colorful mural depicting the history and contributions of Ventura's Chinese population, mark this forgotten era.

of forested slopes, and everywhere there is tranquility, making it clear why the region is a magnet for mystics.

SIGHTS

Since the early 1960s the peaceful rolling hills of Ojai have been recognized for their intense spiritual potential. Today eastern philosophy nests in the heart of the West Coast in secluded centers scattered throughout the rustic landscape.

Set on top of a hill overlooking Ojai Valley is the **Krotona Institute of Theosophy**. This 118-acre forested estate is a center for "students of Theosophy and the ancient wisdom." A spiritual-philosophical movement that developed late in the 19th century, Theosophy combines science with religion and draws from the classic philosopher Pythagoras. Visitors can tour the library, shop in the bookstore, and enjoy the beautifully landscaped grounds. Closed Monday. ~ 2 Krotona Hill, Ojai; 805-646-2653, fax 805-646-7679; www.theosophical.org, e-mail krotona@doc.k.net.

Another sect, the **Krishnamurti Foundation**, has an equally secluded library in the hills on the other side of town. Closed Monday and Tuesday. ~ 1130 McAndrew Road, Ojai; 805-646-4948.

The Pink Moment

If you're visiting Ojai from late October to February, be sure to be outside as sunset approaches to catch what's known as the Pink Moment. The rays of the setting sun turn the Topa Topa Mountains a rosy pink. It's a spectacular sight, especially if you can share it with someone special.

At nearby **Meditation Mount**, where the grounds and meditation rooms are open daily, there are special community meditative sessions to celebrate the full moon. ~ 10340 Reeves Road, Ojai; 805-646-5508, fax 805-646-3303; www.meditation.com, e-mail meditation@meditation.com.

Before venturing to these ethereal heights, stop off at the **Ojai Valley Chamber of Commerce and Visitor's Bureau**, which has maps and brochures of the area. Closed Tuesday. ~ 150 West Ojai Avenue, Ojai; 805-646-8126, fax 805-646-9762; www.ojaichamber.org, e-mail info@ojaichamber.org.

Just steps away, the **Ojai Valley Museum** inhabits a 1919 mission-style church. The former churchyard now boasts a Chumash interpretive garden, a lush collection of medicinal and comestible plants. Inside, you'll find exhibits focusing on the Hispanic and Chumash history of the region, with ceramics, basketry, furniture, and photographs on display. Closed Monday and Tuesday. Admission. ~ 130 West Ojai Avenue; 805-640-1390; www.ojaivalleymuseum.org, e-mail ojaivalleymuseum@ojai.net.

The 1917 mission revival **Post Office** is also downtown. ~ 201 East Ojai Avenue, Ojai. While you are there, visit the Spanish-style **City Hall**. You'll find a secluded garden there. ~ 401 South Ventura Street, Ojai; 805-646-5581, fax 805-646-1980.

To capture the spirit of Ojai, hike, bicycle, or drive the back roads and mountain lanes. Grand Avenue loop will carry you past orange orchards and horse ranches to the foot of the mountains. It leads along thick stone walls built by Chinese laborers during the 19th century. ~ Take Ojai Avenue, Route 150, east from town; turn left on Reeves Road, left again on McAndrew Road, left on Thacher Road, and left on Carne Road. This returns to Route 150, completing the ten-mile loop.

East End Drive follows Route 150 west past palm trees and farmhouses. Three miles from town, on a promontory with a stone bench inscribed "The Ojai Valley," is the overlook from which actor Ronald Colman gazed down on Shangri-La in *Lost Horizon*. With deep green orchards below and sharp gold mountains above, it truly evokes that fictional utopia.

The highway winds high into the sun-scorched mountains past forests of pine and oak. Paralleling the Sespe River, Route 33 bisects rocky defiles and skirts 7500-foot Reyes Peak. For 60 miles the road tracks through the mountains until it meets Route 166, where the alternatives are heading east to the Central Valley or west toward the coastline.

LODGING

Ojai Valley Inn & Spa

905 Country Club Road
805-646-5511, 800-422-6524, fax 805-646-7969
www.ojairesort.com, e-mail info@ojairesort.com
300 rooms
ULTRA-DELUXE

Set in a pastoral valley with spectacular mountain vistas and shaded by mature California coast live oaks, the 220-acre Ojai Valley Inn & Spa has been around in some form or another since the 1920s. Currently the resort is undergoing a major renovation, due to be completed in early 2005. The spa, restaurant, adjoining hotel rooms, and the golf course are open during the ongoing construction, with swimming pool, additional rooms, and restaurants opening as they are completed. The resort features a stunning multi-court tennis center and offers some of California's premier hiking trails and treks on horseback.

Rose Garden Inn
615 West Ojai Avenue
805-646-1434, 800-799-1881, fax 805-640-8455
www.rosegardeninn.com, e-mail info@rosegardeninn.com
17 rooms
MODERATE TO DELUXE

The 17-unit Rose Garden Inn offers comfort at reasonable prices. The large attractive rooms are paneled in knotty cedar with floors carpeted wall to wall. All rooms include refrigerators and microwaves; some have fireplaces. Outside a clean spacious pool, whirlpool, and sauna complete this inn's reputation as a perfect summer getaway. A full complimentary breakfast is included in the rate.

Spa Heaven

Ringed by craggy mountain peaks and carpeted by native flowers, the Ojai Valley is an inspirational spot. Perhaps that's why two of California's finest day spas nestle here, providing an array of special services that draw on the area's natural beauty. Along with traditional spa treatments such as waxing and massage, **The Oaks at Ojai** leads guests on a variety of town and mountain hikes. **The Ojai Valley Inn & Spa** offers art classes inspired by local flora, as well as healing treatments influenced by indigenous Chumash practices.

The Oaks at Ojai
122 East Ojai Avenue
805-646-5573, 800-753-6257, fax 805-640-1504
www.oaksspa.com, e-mail info@oaksspa.com
42 rooms
DELUXE

Because of its surrounding mountains Ojai is extremely popular with the health conscious. One of the region's leading spas, The Oaks at Ojai, caters to this interest. It provides a full menu of physical activity including aerobic exercise, weight training, yoga classes, body conditioning, and massage. Guests take all their meals—low-calorie vegetarian, fish, or poultry plates—at the spa. The accommodations include comfortable, spacious rooms in the lodge and multi-unit cottages dotting the grounds. Included in the tab are three meals, fitness classes, and use of the pool, saunas, jacuzzi, and other health facilities.

DINING

Ranch House

South Lomita Avenue
805-646-2360
www.theranchhouse.com
dinner and Sunday brunch only; closed Monday
DELUXE TO ULTRA-DELUXE

Everyone's favorite Ojai restaurant is the Ranch House. Little wonder since this dining terrace rests in a

tranquil garden surrounded by ferns, bamboo, and rose bushes. A flowering hedge shelters one side while a statue of Buddha gazes out from the other. Nearby, a graceful footbridge curves across a koi pond. Dinner includes venison tenderloin, grilled diver scallops, freshwater striped bass, and veal in cream sauce. Desserts come from the restaurant's bakery, as do the three varieties of bread served with each meal.

L'Auberge

314 El Paseo Road
805-646-2288
www.laubergeojai.com
lunch on weekends only; dinner served daily
MODERATE TO DELUXE

For fine French–Belgian dining L'Auberge, a venerable old house replete with brick fireplace and chandeliers, sets the tone. You can also dine on the terrace, choosing from a menu that includes scampi, frogs' legs, poached sole, tournedos, pepper steak, sweetbreads, and duckling in orange sauce. Lunch, served only on weekends, features almost a dozen different crêpes.

SHOPPING

The center of the shopping scene in the mountain resort town of Ojai is **Arcade Plaza**, a promenade between Ojai Avenue and Matilija Street that extends from Montgomery Street to Signal Street. Within this tile-roofed warren and along surrounding blocks are crafts stores and galleries. Many are operated by the community of artisans that has grown over the years in Ojai.

An even more extensive collection of pottery is on display at the **Human Arts Gallery.** There are also paintings, handblown glass pieces, and handwrought jewelry items. ~ 310 East Ojai Avenue; 805-646-1525.

Pottery Personae

In a hilltop estate flanked by gardens lies the **Beatrice Wood Studio**, a place that you absolutely must visit. Beatrice Wood, whose autobiography is titled *I Shock Myself*, was a regional institution until her death in 1998 at age 105. Tremendously talented, she was a potter for six decades. Her work shows incredible range. Pieces are wrought as figurines of people and animals: vases feature forms in bas-relief; pitchers are shaped as people, their arms pouring spouts; couples are cast in bed or standing forlornly. The studio houses a permanent collection and a gift shop. Open by appointment only. ~ 8560 Ojai-Santa Paula Road, Ojai; 805-646-3381; www.beatricewood.com, e-mail info@beatricewood.com.

HIDDEN

Arts Alliance

Given the number of creative types hanging around Ojai, it's not surprising that **Local Hero Bookstore** is a major showcase for local talent. This friendly bookstore hosts live music every Friday night and readings every Saturday afternoon. The café in back serves beer, wine, and a variety of espresso drinks. ~ 254 East Ojai Avenue, Ojai; 805-646-3165; www.localherobooks.com.

For stylish fashions, visit the **Barbara Bowman Shops**, owned by the well-known designer. ~ 125 and 133 East Ojai Avenue; 805-646-2970.

Primavera Gallery showcases a fine collection of glass, including a series of handpainted chandeliers by Ulla Darni. ~ 214 East Ojai Avenue, Ojai; 805-646-7133; www.primaveraart.com.

For museum-quality traditional pottery, head east from town to **The Pottery**. Otto Heino has been working in porcelain and stoneware for decades. After browsing the showroom visitors can wander the landscaped grounds viewing the carp pond, cactus garden, and peacocks. Closed Monday. ~ 971 McAndrew Road, Ojai; 805-646-3393.

NIGHTLIFE

There's live rock, jazz, or blues at the **Ojai Brew Pub** on Friday and Saturday nights. Wednesday night is open-mic night, so there's no telling what entertainment to expect. ~ 423 East Ojai Avenue #101, Ojai; 805-646-8837; www.ojaibrewpub.com.

World Famous Deer Lodge Tavern & Restaurant, a jukebox-and-pool-table bar, has dancing to rhythm-and-blues and rock bands every Friday and Saturday. Occasional cover. ~ 2261 Route 33, Ojai; 805-646-4256.

PARKS

Lake Casitas Recreation Area is a 6200-acre park surrounded by forested slopes and featuring a many-fingered lake. No swimming is permitted since Casitas is a reservoir, but fishing and boating are encouraged. Outlying mountains and the proximity of Ojai make it a particularly popular locale. Facilities include picnic areas, restrooms, showers, a snack bar, a bait-and-tackle shop, and a grocery store. For bike rentals and boat rentals, call 805-649-2043. Bass, trout, and channel catfish are caught in these waters. Day-use fee, $6.50 per vehicle. ~11311 Santa Ana Road about ten miles east of Ventura; 805-649-2233, fax 805-649-4661.

Camping: There are 400 tent/RV sites in total, 156 with hookups. Camping costs $22 to $44 with hookups, $16 to $18 without.

6.

North of Santa Barbara

North of Santa Barbara the landscape turns from urban to rural, as pockets of commerce are replaced by rolling grasslands and stunning ocean views. The valleys are rimmed by rugged mountains, and there are plenty of beaches, parks, and wide open spaces for hiking, biking, horseback riding, and simply hanging out.

Past the bedroom community of Goleta and the University of California, Highway 101 snakes past pretty ranch lands and dazzling views of the sparkling Pacific. Along the way there are state parks with broad expanses of undeveloped beaches to explore.

When the road turns inland, it's a short detour to Lompoc, known for its flower fields, Air Force base, and historic mission.

Still mainly an agricultural community, the city's farming history is depicted in the murals that adorn the public buildings around town, while its mission-era history is centered around La Purísima Mission. Destroyed by an earthquake in 1812, the mission was completely rebuilt in the 1930s on the original site.

Further inland, Santa Ynez Valley's towns are surrounded by ranches, farms, and vineyards. Much of the region is horse country. Stud farms and working ranches dot the countryside and thoroughbreds graze in the meadows. For years this was a quiet area, mostly populated by those looking for some breathing room, but in recent years the farms have turned into more profitable vineyards, introducing a rising number of gentlemen farmers. The formerly simple farm towns of Santa Ynez and Los Olivos have become quite chi-chi, with gourmet restaurants, tiny bou-

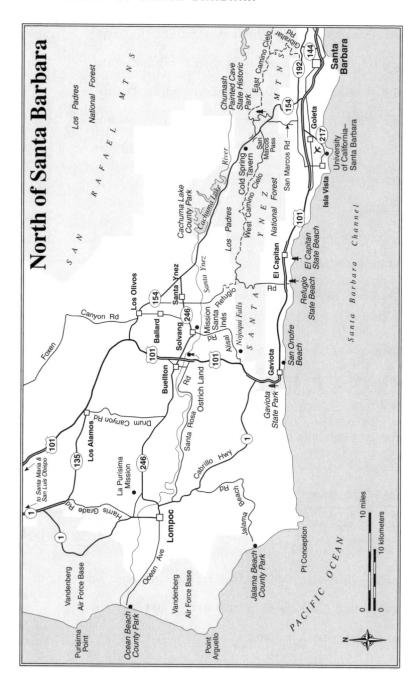

North of Santa Barbara

tiques, perfectly decorated inns, and even day spas. And for kitsch there's nothing quite as over the top as Solvang, offering a sugar-coated taste of Denmark in the midst of farm country.

Goleta Valley Area

Goleta is Santa Barbara's practical counterpart. Though the town was officially established in 1875, with the arrival of its first post office, it didn't find a spot on the map until the 1950s, when the University of California, aerospace companies, and housing developments turned it into a Santa Barbara suburb. Today this is where high-tech companies flourish, university students call home, and moms and pops raise their kids. What keeps it from the strictly mundane is its proximity to some lovely stretches of coast and beachside parks.

University of California–Santa Barbara.

SIGHTS

The main attraction in this coastal area is the **University of California–Santa Barbara**, a Nobel Laureate–rich campus (UCSB faculty includes three Nobel Prize winners in chemistry and physics) spread across 989 acres along the California coastline. The University sits on the foundation of Santa Barbara's old coastal fort and boasts one of the most spectacular strips of beach in Santa Barbara, including Campus Point, Sands Beach, and Oil Point. Take a stroll from Storke Tower, at the center of campus, around the University's saltwater lagoon, and out to the rugged cliffs of Campus Point. Also be sure to tour some of the museums and galleries scattered throughout the campus.

Stop by the visitors center to pick up a campus map and brochures for one of the state's most beautiful universities, or join a guided tour. Closed weekends. ~ 805-893-2487, fax 805-893-8610; www.ucsb.edu.

Hit the Beach, Not the Books

When the founders of UCSB chose the secluded spot along the Goleta coast to build the campus, they didn't realize that mixing sun, sea, and some of Santa Barbara's finest surfing might be counterproductive to academics. Simply named "Campus Point," UCSB's headland that protrudes into the Pacific is a favorite spot for locals, the occasional visitor, and students who most likely should be in class. Receiving "ride-able" waves about 190 days out of the year, the point stands as a great place for beginners as well as veteran boarders. When the waves are really charging, the rides can carry on for nearly a mile.

Bacara Resort
& Spa.

Cutting a swath between mountains and ocean, the road passes a series of attractive beach parks, then turns inland toward the mountains and interior valleys.

LODGING

Bacara Resort & Spa
8301 Holister Avenue
805-968-0100, 877-422-4245, fax 805-968-1800
www.bacararesort.com, e-mail info@bacararesort.com
360 rooms
ULTRA-DELUXE

Ocean views, lush landscaping, and quintessential Santa Barbara red-tile architecture highlight Bacara Resort & Spa, a property tucked into the ocean bluffs north of Santa Barbara. Over 300 guest rooms and 49 suites, each with balcony or private patio, spread over 78 palm-fringed acres. The guest quarters are so tastefully appointed you might not want to leave your room. But

The Writing on the Wall

Rare and intricate cave paintings by Chumash Indians decorate the sandstone walls at **Chumash Painted Cave State Historic Park**. Strange animal and human figures, as well as various abstract shapes, appear in vivid red, white, and black colors. The oldest paintings here are thought to be 1000 years old, but some of them are quite recent. The Chumash still consider their art sacred—these paintings are one of the only examples on view to the public. ~ On Painted Caves Road, three miles south of San Marcos Pass. Take Route 154 out of Santa Barbara and turn right on Painted Caves Road. The cave is on the left, up a narrow, steep road. *Warning:* Trailers and RVs should not attempt this road.

then you'd miss the three swimming pools, four tennis courts, top-rated golf course, and nearby hiking trails, not to mention the full-service spa with its rejuvenating treatments and classes. This and much more make Bacara the picture-perfect escape—that is, if you have deep pockets.

El Capitan Canyon
11560 Calle Real, Goleta
805-685-3887, 866-352-2729, fax 805-968-6772
www.elcapitancanyon.com, e-mail info@elcapitancanyon.com
100 cabins, 26 tents
MODERATE TO ULTRA-DELUXE

If you want to spend the night in the great outdoors and wake up smelling the scent of the woods, but yearn to sleep on rich linens, soak in jacuzzi tubs, and be pampered, check into El Capitan Canyon. Located about 20 miles north of Santa Barbara, about a half mile inland from El Capitan State Beach, this luxury campground offers a variety of cabins and tent cabins. This sprawling 100-acre complex, whose goal is "to nurture an environment in harmony with the nature and history of the Canyon," features picnic areas, restrooms, showers, a store, a pool, a playground, game areas, and an outdoor theater that has live music on Saturday. The Equestrian Center at El Capitan Ranch has guided horseback rides through the foothills of the coastal Santa Ynez Mountains. It's not your typical campground experience, but it might satisfy the fussiest potential camper in your group.

DINING

Miró
Bacara Resort & Spa
8301 Holister Avenue
805-968-0100, 877-422-4245, fax 805-968-1800
www.bacararesort.com, e-mail info@bacararesort.com
ULTRA-DELUXE

*Miró at Bacara
Resort & Spa.*

A visit to Miró, Bacara Resort's signature restaurant, is a treat for the senses. The healthy menu features organic produce, freshly caught seafood, and the tenderest meats and poultry available. In addition to exceptional food, they serve fine wines from their premium wine cellar. The decor, inspired by artist Joan Miró, tantalizes the eyes; his use of colors and shapes resonate throughout the dining room. Original sculptures by the renowned artist adorn the facility. And then, to top it off, there's the setting: a bluff overlooking the Pacific. A picture-perfect place for a romantic splurge.

NIGHTLIFE

Head into the mountains about 27 miles outside Santa Barbara and catch a show at the **Circle Bar B Dinner Theatre**. This well-known facility has a menu of comedies and musicals. Open weekends only from April through October. ~ 1800 Refugio Road, 27 miles north of Santa Barbara; 805-967-1962; www.circlebarbtheatre.com.

BEACHES & PARKS

El Capitan State Beach is another one of Southern California's sparkling beaches, stretching along three miles of oceanfront. The 168-acre park features a nature trail, tidepools, and wonderful opportunities for hiking along the beach. El Capitan Creek, fringed by oak and sycamore trees, traverses the area. Seals and sea lions often romp offshore, and in winter gray whales cruise by. This is a good place for swimming, surfing (off El Capitan Point), and catching grunion. Facilities include picnic areas, restrooms, showers, a store, and seasonal lifeguards. Day-use fee, $5. ~ Located in Goleta off Route 101, about 20 miles north of Santa Barbara; 805-968-1033.

El Capitan
State Beach.

Refugio State Beach.

Camping: There are 140 tent/RV sites (no hookups) in the park near the beach; $21 per night. Reservations: 800-444-7275.

Refugio State Beach is a 39-acre park with over a mile of ocean frontage. You can bask on a sandy beach, lie under palm trees on the greensward, and hike or bicycle along the two-and-a-half-mile path that connects this park with El Capitan. There are also interesting tidepools. Facilities include picnic areas, restrooms, showers, seasonal lifeguard, and a store. Fishing, swimming, and surfing are good. Day-use fee, $5. ~ Located on Refugio Road off Route 101, about 23 miles north of Santa Barbara; 805-968-1033.

Camping: There are 82 tent/RV sites (no hookups); $21 per night. Reservations: 800-444-7275.

The nudist haven of **San Onofre Beach** is a rare find. Frequented by few people, it is a pretty white-sand beach that winds along rocky headlands. There's not much here except beautiful views, shore plant life, and savvy sunbathers. Wander for miles past cliffs and coves. ~ Located off Route 101 about 30 miles north of Santa Barbara and two miles south of Gaviota. Driving north on Route 101, make a U-turn on Vista del Mar Road; drive south on Route 101 for seven-tenths of a mile to a dirt parking area. Cross the railroad tracks; a path next to the railroad light signal leads to the beach.

Further up the coast you will find **Gaviota State Park**, a mammoth 2776-acre facility that stretches along both sides of Route 101. The beach rests in a sandy cove guarded on either side by dramatic sedimentary rock formations. A railroad trestle traverses the beach and a fishing pier extends offshore. Facilities include picnic areas, restrooms, showers, and lifeguards. Day-use fee, $5. ~ The beach is located off Route 101, about 30 miles northwest of Santa Barbara; 805-968-1033.

Camping: There are 40 tent/RV sites (no hookups); $14 per night. The vegetation is sparse from the forest fires a few years ago, and there is no drinking water, so bring your own. Sites are first-come, first-served.

The remote **Jalama Beach County Park** sits at the far end of a 14-mile-long country road. Nevertheless, in summer there are likely to be many campers here. They come for the broad sandy beach fringed by coastal bluffs and undulating hills. Jalama Creek cuts through the park,

Pier near Goleta.

Rural Rambling

About 35 miles from Santa Barbara Routes 101 and 1 diverge. For a rural drive past white barns and meandering creeks, follow Route 1. En route to Lompoc it passes farmlands, pastures, and rolling hills. About five miles south of Lompoc, you can follow **Jalama Road**, a country lane that cuts through sharp canyons and graceful valleys on a winding 15-mile course to the ocean, ending at a beach park. Stay on Route 1, and you'll encounter **La Purísima Mission**. The best restored of all 21 California missions, this historic site has an eerie way of projecting you back to Spanish days. There's the mayordomo's abode with the table set and a pan on the stove, and the mission store, its barrels overflowing with corn and beans. The entire mission complex, from the church to the tallow vats where the fat from slaughtered cattle was rendered into soap, was re-created in the 1930s by the Civilian Conservation Corps. Founded nearby in 1787, the mission was re-established at this site in 1813. Today you can tour the living quarters of priests, soldiers, and Indians, the workshops where weaving, leathermaking, and carpentry were practiced, and the mission's original water system. You can also see animals such as burros and goats in their period mission setting. Living-history events occur here periodically; call ahead for details. Admission. ~ 2295 Purísima Road, Lompoc; 805-733-3713, fax 805-733-2497.

creating a wetland frequented by the endangered California brown pelican. Point Conception lies a few miles to the south, and the area all around is undeveloped and quite pretty (though Vandenberg Air Force Base is situated north of the beach). This is a good area for beachcombing as well as rock-hounding for chert, agate, travertine, and fossils. Facilities include picnic areas, restrooms, hot showers, a store, a snack bar, and a playground. Swimming is not recommended because of dangerous rip currents; there are no lifeguards stationed here. Surfing is good at Tarantula Point about a half mile south of the park. You can surf-fish for perch or fish from the rocky points for cabezon and rock fish. Day-use fee, $6. ~ From Lompoc take Route 1 south for five miles; turn onto Jalama Beach Road and follow it 15 miles to the end; 805-736-3504, fax 805-735-8020.

Camping: There are 110 tent/RV sites (28 with electrical hookups); $18 to $25 per night.

Santa Ynez Mountains The mountain road

from Santa Barbara, Route 154, curves up into the Santa Ynez Mountains past forests of evergreen and oak. All

along the roadside are rocky promontories with broad views back toward the city and out over the ocean.

Turn off onto Stagecoach Road, head downhill a mile, and rein in at **Cold Spring Tavern**, smack dab between Santa Barbara and Santa Ynez Valley. Back in the 1880s this squat wood structure served as a rest stop

for stagecoaches coming through San Marcos Pass. Next door is a split-log cabin with a stone fireplace. ~ 5995 Stagecoach Road, off Route 154, Santa Barbara; 805-967-0066, fax 805-964-5995; www.coldspringtavern.com.

Beyond the mountain pass, amid striated hills and rolling ranch country, lies **Cachuma Lake**. Fed by creeks from Los Padres National Forest, this eight-mile-long lake is a jewel to the eye. Boating and fishing facilities lie nearby, and hiking trails lead into the nearby wilderness. Day-use fee, $6. ~ 805-686-5054; www.cachuma.com.

LODGING

Rancho Oso Guest Ranch and Stables
3750 Paradise Road, Santa Barbara
805-683-5686, fax 805-683-5111
www.rancho-oso.com, e-mail rosh@1000trails.com
MODERATE

Before reaching Cachuma Lake and Santa Ynez, veer off 154 onto Paradise Road to get lost in the Old West. Rancho Oso Guest Ranch and Stables is isolated in the mountains of Santa Barbara next to Los Padres National Forest, and beckons your inner frontiersman. You can ride the range then camp out in Conestoga covered wagons (electricity provided), or check into cabins that feature Western facades but are stocked with coffee makers and small refrigerators. If

Rancho Oso Guest Ranch and Stables.

you want to drive up in your RV or bring your own steed along, you're quite welcome. Guided trail rides are offered at their stables (805-683-5110). Rancho Oso offers a heated pool and spa to soak those weary bones (that's my kind of roughing it!), and the Stone Lodge Kitchen & Chuckwagon serves family-style meals on weekends and holidays.

DINING & NIGHTLIFE

Cold Spring Tavern
5995 Stagecoach Road, off Route 154, Santa Barbara
805-967-0066, fax 805-964-5995
www.coldspringtavern.com
DELUXE TO ULTRA-DELUXE.

A vestige of the Old West, Cold Spring Tavern is a former stagecoach stop dating back to the 19th century. The floors tilt, the bar is wood plank, and the walls are stained with a century of use; a cow head with antlers crowns the stone fireplace. Dinner in this roughhewn time capsule features marinated rabbit, steak, pork back ribs, and fresh seafood. The evening special might be elk or buffalo, but that is a rare occasion. At lunch you can order a venison steak sandwich, chile verde, or a buffalo burger. Make a point of stopping by. Dinner reservations are recommended. Breakfast is served on weekends.

Carousing at Cold Spring Tavern is like being in an old Western movie. Every Friday night and Saturday and Sunday afternoons you can pull up a stool and listen to

Cachuma Lake.

Horse-Drawn History

Anchoring the Western facades of Santa Ynez to the 19th century, the **Janeway Carriage House** (or Santa Ynez Valley

Historical Society Museum and Carriage House) boasts a collection of memorabilia from the Old West, along with an extensive showroom of horse-drawn buggies and carriages. Step into the past to view horse-drawn fire carriages and classic Wells Fargo/U.S. Mail carriers. Closed Monday and Tuesday. ~ 3596 Sagunto Street, Santa Ynez; 805-688-7889, fax 805-688-1109; www.syvm.org.

the rock, country-and-western, and rhythm-and-blues bands that ride through.

PARKS

Surrounded by the 4000-foot Santa Ynez Mountains and 6000-foot San Rafael Mountains, **Cachuma Lake County Park** holds one of the prettiest lakes along the entire Central Coast. Oak forests and fields of tall grass border much of the shoreline. It's a great place for families and people exploring the backcountry above Santa Barbara. The many amenities include picnic areas, restrooms, a swimming pool, a snack bar, a store, a nature center (805-688-4515), a boat launch and rentals (805-688-4040), lake cruises (805-686-5050, 805-686-5055 on weekends), seasonal bike rentals, a par course, a game field, and hiking trails. Swimming is not permitted in lake, but there is a pool (open summer only). The lake has trout, perch, bass, bluegill, crappie, and catfish. Day-use fee, $6 per vehicle. ~ Located north of Santa Barbara on Route 154; 805-688-4658; www.cachuma.com.

Camping: There are 350 tent sites ($18 per night), 35 partial hookups ($25 per night), and 150 full hookups ($25 per night). Sites are first-come, first-served.

Santa Ynez Valley
Thirty miles from Santa Barbara the mountains open onto the Santa Ynez Valley. Here a string of sleepy towns creates a Western-style counterpoint to California's chic coastline. The first town along 154 from Santa Barbara is Santa Ynez. Located between empty rolling hills and the vaulting Santa Ynez Mountain range, this small town of Western facades and quiet residents is rapidly changing. Originally an outpost for ranchers and those looking to escape the sea and city, Santa Ynez is quickly turning into Santa Barbara County's premier wine-growing region.

Ballard is a block-long town that was settled in 1880 and features the **Ballard School**, a little red schoolhouse that was constructed a few years later. ~ 2425 School Street, Ballard.

As you travel up toward the valley's end you'll come to **Los Olivos**. Similar to its neighbors in size and feel, Los Olivos has embraced a bit more of Santa Barbara's chicness. Los Olivos is complete with a white steeple church that dates back to 1897. It is also home to **Mattei's Tavern**, a former stagecoach inn constructed in 1886. This fine old

woodframe building has a trellised porch. ~ Route 154, Los Olivos; 805-688-4820.

LODGING

Santa Ynez Inn

3627 Sagunto Street, Santa Ynez
805-688-5588, 800-643-5774, fax 805-686-4294
www.santaynezinn.com, e-mail info@santa
ynezinn.com
14 rooms
ULTRA-DELUXE

If you're a fan of creature comforts, try the stand-out Victorian mansion at the edge of town. The Santa Ynez Inn's 19th-century furnishings combine with 21st-century features like a heated whirlpool to make your stay memorable and comfortable. Fourteen elegantly decorated rooms all come with private baths, plush

Stress Buster

Sunset spas for couples, Thai yoga massages for the adventurous, and rejuvenating treatments for the weary may all be had when **Spa Vigne** teams up with Fess Parker's Inn to create that special weekend retreat. Many treatments make use of local products, such as crushed grapeseeds and wine infusions, to enhance their effectiveness. And don't forget Fido—you can also book a doggie massage, good for relieving all that built-up canine stress. ~ 2971 Grand Avenue, Los Olivos; 805-688-7323.

beds, refrigerators, coffee pots, and air conditioning for the valley's summer months. Some rooms also boast romantic fireplaces.

Fess Parker's Wine Country Inn and Spa

2860 Grand Avenue, Los Olivos
805-688-7788, 800-446-2455, fax 805-688-1942
www.fessparker.com, e-mail infoinn@fessparker.com
14 rooms
ULTRA-DELUXE

Located in the middle of Los Olivos, Fess Parker's Wine Country Inn and Spa is an oasis for relaxation set in two country-style buildings. The 14 rooms feature fireplaces and down beds, making them a perfect setting for the complimentary breakfast in bed. Wine and cheese is served every evening. For a personal touch, each guest room has been decorated by Marcy Parker. Hotel amenities include a pool, a hot tub, free winetasting, and complimentary use of mountain bikes.

DINING

The Vineyard House
3631 Sagunto Street, Santa Ynez
805-688-2886, fax 805-693-1659
www.thevineyardhouse.com
DELUXE

The Vineyard House, located next door to the Santa Ynez Inn, offers the best atmosphere in town (and some say the best food). Owners Jim and Debbie Sobell have matched California cuisine with Southern flair, and there's something for everyone, from seafood ravioli and shrimp scampi to mouth-watering filet mignon. The indoor dining rooms are quiet and upscale, or you can dine casually on the restaurant's lovely front porch.

Los Olivos Café
2879 Grand Avenue, Los Olivos
805-688-7265, fax 805-688-5953
DELUXE

For those with refined tastes, Los Olivos Café offers the best dining choice in this sleepy town. Its chic atmosphere compliments the Mediterranean cuisine. Enjoy tastes from their extensive wine collection while sitting beneath leafy vines on the rustic terrace. You can start with baked brie or bruschetta rustica and finish with an Italian specialty like chicken piccata, lamb shank or hand-

stuffed ravioli. The restaurant also features "Wednesday with the Wine Maker," when local vineyards come to strut their stuff. A $10 charge includes hors d'oeuvres.

Mattei's Tavern
2350 Railway Avenue, Los Olivos
805-688-4820
DELUXE

Santa Ynez Valley Wineries

The Santa Ynez Valley is a prime winegrowing region with several dozen wineries scattered around the valley. Tucked in the golden hills just south of Santa Ynez is the **Sunstone Winery**. This vintner draws local crowds from Santa Barbara every weekend, offering sauvignon blanc and viognier tasting in a sun-baked courtyard. Merlots and other reds are served in the back room of the earthy, adobe-style villa. Tasting fee. ~ 125 Refugio Road, Santa Ynez; 805-688-9463, fax 805-686-1881; www.sunstonewinery.com.

Another winetasting stop along 154, between Los Olivos and Santa Ynez, is the **Bridlewood Winery**, a perfect place to pull over and enjoy a rest. This tranquil, mission-style winery beckons guests to enjoy glasses of chardonnay, viognier, syrah, and cabernet from their porches or at patio tables overlooking a glassy lake and rolling vineyards. Tasting fee. ~ 3555 Roblar Road, Santa Ynez; 805-688-9000, fax 805-688-2443; www. bridlewoodwinery.com.

For a long country ride, travel out Zaca Station and Foxen Canyon roads in Los Olivos. A string of wineries begins with the

There's yet another stagecoach-stop-turned-restaurant in the Santa Ynez Valley. Mattei's Tavern is a mammoth old building that served as an inn back in the 1880s. Today you can dine in a rustically decorated room or out on the patio. Dinner features steaks, prime rib, pasta, and fresh seafood dishes. For a sense of history and a good meal, it's a safe bet. Reservations are recommended. Dinner only.

most elegant. **Firestone Vineyard** is set in stone-trimmed buildings and features a courtyard and picnic areas. The largest winery in the valley, it offers several estate-grown varietal wines. Tasting fee. ~ 5000 Zaca Station Road, Los Olivos; 805-688-3940; www.firestonewine.com, e-mail info@firestonewine.com.

Zaca Mesa Winery sits about nine miles from Route 101 in a modern woodframe building with an attractive tasting room; it's a beautiful winery with vineyards lining Foxen Canyon Road. Other wineries lie farther along the road and throughout the Santa Ynez Valley. ~ 6905 Foxen Canyon Road, Los Olivos; 805-688-3310, 800-350-7972; www.zacamesa.com, e-mail zmail@zacamesa.com.

The **Buttonwood Winery** is a small winery that bottles sauvignon blanc, semillon, marsanne, merlot, cabernet sauvignon, and franc and syrah. This family business turns out well-regarded wine under the Kalyra label. ~ 1500 Alamo Pintado Road, Solvang; 805-688-3032; www.buttonwoodwinery.com.

The **Rideau Winery**, just north of Solvang, adds a dash of Southern flavor to the wine country. The owner, Iris Rideau, blends the California landscape with a rich, Southern-style garden: shaded lawns, intimate country tasting rooms, and covered porches. Rideau features a variety of wines such as tempranillo, reserve viognier, and their award-winning white riesling. Tasting fee. ~ 1562 Alamo Pintado Road, Solvang; 805-688-0717; www.rideauvineyard.com.

SHOPPING

Driving down Santa Ynez's main strip, Sagunto Street, you'll come across the women's clothing boutique **Anna** nestled among Western-style storefronts. This shop offers the latest fashions from New York to Milan at reasonable

prices. ~ 3569 Sagunto Street, Santa Ynez; 805-693-8050; www.anna couture.com.

Located just east of Anna, **J. Woeste Home and Garden** is a cozy, country-style showroom filled with unique decorations for both indoors and gardens, including ornate flower pots and iron bird cages. Closed Sunday and Monday. ~ 3605 Sagunto Street, Santa Ynez; 805-688-0992.

In **Los Olivos**, several art galleries and antique shops help round out your shopping spree.

Solvang The valley's most famous town does not resemble any of the others. In fact, it doesn't really resemble any real town in California. Solvang looks like it was designed by Walt Disney. The place is a Danish village complete with cobblestone walks, gaslights, and stained-glass windows. Steep-pitched roofs with high dormers create an Old World atmosphere here. Stores and homes showcase the tall, narrow architecture of Scandinavia, and windmills dominate the view. What saves the place from being a theme park is that Solvang actually *is* a Danish town. Emigrants from Denmark established a village and school here in 1911. For visitors, wandering around Solvang means catching a ride on a horse-drawn Danish streetcar, then popping into a Danish bakery for hot pretzels or *aebleskiver*, a tasty Danish pastry.

SIGHTS

Bethania Lutheran Church illustrates Danish provincial architecture. The model of a fully rigged ship hanging

Mission Santa Inés.

from the ceiling is traditional to Scandinavian churches. ~ At Atterdag Roadand Laurel Avenue, Solvang.

To further confuse things, the centerpiece of Solvang in no way fits the architecture of the town. **Mission Santa Inés** does, however, meet the building style of the rest of California. Founded in 1804, the mission church follows the long, narrow, rectangular shape common in Spanish California. The altar is painted brilliant colors and the colonnaded courtyard is ablaze with flowers. A small museum displays 18th-century bibles and song books, and one chapel contains a 17th-century statue made of polychrome wood. ~ On Mission Drive, Solvang.

To escape the bustle of Solvang, take a ride out on **Alisal Road**. After six miles this rustic road arrives at **Nojoqui Falls**. There's a picnic park here and a short hiking trail up to hillside cascades.

"Hog" historians will get a kick out of the **Vintage Motorcycle Museum**. Located at the south edge of Solvang, this museum boasts a showroom of mint-condition bikes ranging from an 1886 Benz replica and original 1904 NSU to present-day speed-demons. Open Saturday and Sunday and by appointment only. Admission. ~ 320

Get Your Head Out of the Sand

Between Solvang and Buellton (on Route 246) lies a hidden gem, **Ostrich Land.** This funky big-bird farm gives children and adults the chance to get up close and personal with herds of ostriches and emus. The ostriches, sometimes over six feet tall, are quite a sight. The owner encourages you to feed the birds, as long as you hide any shiny objects—these birds will peck at anything. ~ 610 East Route 246, Buellton; 805-686-9696; www.ostrich land.com, e-mail ostri@ostrichland.com.

Alisal Road, Solvang; 805-686-9522; www.motosolvang.
com, e-mail info@motosolvang.com.

LODGING

Alisal Guest Ranch
1054 Alisal Road, Solvang
805-688-6411, 800-425-4725, fax 805-688-2510
www.alisal.com, e-mail sales@alisal.com
ULTRA-DELUXE

Up in the Santa Ynez Valley, tucked between the
Santa Ynez and San Rafael mountains, lies Alisal Guest
Ranch. A 10,000-acre working cattle ranch, Alisal represents one of the original Spanish land grants. Part of the
ranch is an exclusive resort featuring 73 units, two 18-
hole golf courses, a swimming pool, a spa, tennis courts,
and a dining room. Guests ride horseback through the
property and fish and sail on a mile-long lake. Square
dances, hay rides, and summer barbecue dinners add to
the entertainment. Breakfast and dinner are included.

Solvang Gardens Lodge
293 Alisal Road, Solvang
805-688-4404
www.solvangardens.com, e-mail info@solvangardens.com
BUDGET TO MODERATE

Solvang Gardens Lodge is designed in old Danish style. One room is decorated in floral themes, and many have the warm, knotty-pine walls of a cozy mountain lodge. Several rooms feature kitchens, kitchenettes, and fireplaces. On the grounds are lovely English gardens, a lily pond, waterfalls, and fountains to take in.

DINING

Solvang Bakery
460 Alisal Road, Solvang
805-688-4939
BUDGET

Solvang is famous for its bakeries, and this colorful, sugarcoated pit-stop has excellent Danish pastries and other

Scandinavian treats. It's one of Solvang's most popular attractions, bringing in large weekend crowds that fill up on sweets and carbs.

Hitching Post II
406 East Route 246, Buellton
805-688-0676, 805-686-1946
dinner only
DELUXE TO ULTRA-DELUXE

Just about four miles outside Solvang, the tiny town of Buellton boasts several restaurants serving up locally grown fare. Barbecued artichokes are a tasty way to start your meal at the Hitching Post II, which is well-known for its steaks and barbecue. This popular eatery also serves ostrich—if you haven't tried it, what better place to start?

SHOPPING

Solvang is a choice spot to shop for imported products from Northern Europe. Walk the brick-paved streets and you'll encounter everything from cuckoo clocks to lace curtains. Many of the shops line **Copenhagen Drive.**

There are Danish handknit sweaters, music boxes, tiles, and pewter items. The toy stores are designed to resemble dollhouses, and shops throughout town feature the tile roofs and high gables of Scandinavian stores.

With the feel of a small European village, it's no wonder that Solvang's shopping choices would include antiques. The **Solvang Antique Center** houses 65 different dealers in the Old Mill Shops building. Lovely old things abound every which way you turn. Peruse thousands of baubles, fine furniture, paintings, timepieces, and museum-quality heirloom pieces. ~ 486 1st Street, Solvang; 805-688-6222, fax 805-686-4044; www.solvangantiques.com, e-mail info@solvangantiques.com.

NIGHTLIFE

The **Solvang Theaterfest** is one of the West's oldest repertory groups. Performing during summer months in an open-air theater, it presents musicals and dramas. Box office is closed Monday and Tuesday. ~ 420 2nd Street, Solvang; 805-922-8313, fax 805-922-3074; www.pcpa.org, e-mail pcpa@pcpa.org.

AJ Spurs hosts live music every Friday and Saturday night. This is an elegant Western saloon with log walls, a stone fireplace, and frontier artifacts. ~ 350 East Route 246, Buellton; 805-686-1655; www.ajspurs.com.

Index

Dining and Lodging Index

Lodging Services

Hidden Picture-Perfect Escapes Guides

More Americans than ever before live in large metropolitan areas. So when they want to get away from it all, they go to smaller, quieter, more welcoming spots that leave the traffic and other anxieties of big-city life behind. This series zeros in on just those types of charming getaway spots. By dedicating an entire book to a friendly little destination, each guide is able to offer a variety of features and a depth of coverage unmatched by more general guides.

Hidden Guides

Adventure travel or a relaxing vacation?—"Hidden" guidebooks are the only travel books in the business to provide detailed information on both. Aimed at environmentally aware travelers, our motto is "Where Vacations Meet Adventures." These books combine details on unique hotels, restaurants and sightseeing with information on camping, sports and hiking for the outdoor enthusiast.